FOLLOWING CHRIST

A HANDBOOK OF CATHOLIC MORAL TEACHING

Daniel L. Lowery, C.SS.R.

Dedicated to my Redemptorist confreres of the St. Louis Province on the occasion of the two hundred and fiftieth anniversary of our religious family: the Congregation of the Most Holy Redeemer, November 9, 1982.

LIGUORI
PUBLICATIONS

One Liguori Drive
Liguori, Missouri 63057
(314) 464-2500

Imprimi Potest:
John F. Dowd, C.SS.R.
Provincial, St. Louis Province
Redemptorist Fathers

Imprimatur:
Monsignor Edward J. O'Donnell
Vicar General, Archdiocese of St. Louis

ISBN 0-89243-173-3
Library of Congress Catalog Card Number: 82-84373

Cover Design: Pam Hummelsheim

TABLE OF CONTENTS

PART THREE:
LOVE YOUR NEIGHBOR AS YOURSELF

FOREWORD

In the hard school of experience (driving around on back roads) I have learned that it's wise for me to look at a map before starting on a journey. This foreword may serve as a map for you as you begin the journey through these pages. The map is in the form of a few clarifying remarks about the *title* of this book and how the *contents* fit together.

Following Christ: Our highest calling is to follow Christ. The invitation, "Come follow me," repeated so often in the Gospels, extends to all of us. There is no surer way to become fully human and fully Christian than by following Christ. To be sure, following Christ means many things. It means that we *belong* to him. "All of you who have been baptized into Christ have clothed yourselves with him" (Galatians 3:27). It means that we "learn" Christ, which demands "that you must lay aside your former way of life and the old self which deteriorates through illusion and desire, and acquire a fresh, spiritual way of thinking" (Ephesians 4:22-23). It means that we listen to his word and make it part of ourselves. "Let the word of Christ, rich as it is, dwell in you" (Colossians 3:16). It means applying the teaching of Christ to our real lives. "Let us love in deed and in truth and not merely talk about it" (1 John 3:18).

Since this book tries to highlight the moral teaching of Jesus and the demands of discipleship, one of its main sources is of course the Sacred Scripture: that is, in the description of Vatican Council II, "the speech of God as it is put down in writing under the breath of the Holy Spirit" (*Divine Revelation,* 9). As a thirsty man drinks heartily from a flowing fountain, I have tried to draw fresh inspiration from the rich source of the Scriptures, especially the New Testament.

Catholic Moral Teaching: It is clear, however, that the New Testament was never meant to be a complete manual of Christian ethics. This book is based, therefore, on another source of Christian truth — namely, Sacred Tradition: that is, "the Word of God which has been entrusted to the apostles by Christ the Lord and the Holy Spirit" (*Divine Revelation,* 9). This word has been nurtured and developed in the womb of the Church, the Christian community, the Body of Christ.

These two sources, Sacred Scripture and Sacred Tradition, "make up a single sacred deposit of the Word of God, which is entrusted to the Church. By adhering to it the entire holy people, united to its pastors, remains always faithful to the teaching of the apostles, to the brotherhood, to the breaking of bread and to the prayers. (Cf Acts 2:42)" (*Divine Revelation,* 10).

According to Catholic teaching, "the task of giving an authentic interpretation of the Word of God, whether in its written form or in the form of Tradition, has been entrusted to the living teaching office of the Church alone. Its authority in this matter is exercised in the name of Jesus Christ . . . It is clear, therefore, that, in the supremely wise arrangement of God, sacred Tradition, sacred Scripture, and the Magisterium of the Church are so connected and associated that one of them cannot stand without the others . . ." (*Divine Revelation,* 10).

The Second Vatican Council discussed many aspects of the Magisterium of the Church (especially in Chapter 3 of the *Dogmatic Constitution on the Church*). With particular attention to the role of the Magisterium in the moral life, the American bishops summed up: "The Holy Father and the bishops in communion with him have been anointed by the Holy Spirit to be the official and authentic teachers of Christian life . . . It is their office and duty to express the teaching of Christ on moral questions and matters of belief. This special teaching office within the Catholic Church is a gift of the Lord Jesus for the benefit of all his followers in their efforts to know what he teaches, value as he values, and live as free, responsible, loving and holy persons. As Christ says, 'He who hears you, hears me.' The authoritative moral teachings of the Church enlighten personal conscience and are to be regarded as certain and binding norms of morality" (*To Live in Christ Jesus,* 12).

One of the tasks of theologians in the Church is to clarify, explain, and apply these "authoritative moral teachings of the Church." It is a challenging task, especially when dealing with longer and more complex documents, such as papal encyclicals. Theologians are encouraged to study such documents and clarify their teaching according to "the character of the documents in question, or by the frequency by which a certain doctrine is proposed, or by the manner in which the doctrine is formulated" (*The Church*, 25). It is not surprising that at times there will be differences of opinion about the precise meaning or application of a magisterial teaching.

To offer an adequate presentation of "Catholic Moral Teaching" one would, therefore, be expected to gather together the authoritative moral teachings of the Church, provide theological analysis, consult representative theologians, indicate disputed points and the like. *Such a complete treatment is beyond the scope of this book.*

This book takes a far simpler approach. It arises from my conviction that many people look to the Church for moral leadership and yet often do not have the means for discovering what the Church is saying. This book offers to serve, as it were, as a tour guide. It says, in effect, "Would you like to know what the teachers of the Church have said about this moral question or that moral problem? Let me help you . . . ." With this in mind, I have tried to spotlight some of the moral teachings of Vatican Council II; recent papal teachings, especially of Pope John Paul II; teachings of the National Conference of Catholic Bishops; and several recent documents from the Congregation for the Doctrine of the Faith. I have borrowed from some of the great theologians of the past (Saint Augustine, Saint Thomas, Saint Alphonsus) and from some of the great theologians of the present. It is in this simple and modest sense that the "Catholic Moral Teaching" of the title should be understood.

A Handbook: This word in the title is meant to convey what I have said above. I make no pretense of offering a *complete* treatment of moral theology or Christian ethics. Nor do I try to present a thorough theological explanation or defense of many of the things that are said in these pages. A handbook is not a theological treatise, but a concise and convenient summary of major themes. Considered in that light, a handbook can be helpful.

The *contents* of this book are arranged according to a familiar pattern. From apostolic times until our own, there have been innumerable efforts to organize and communicate the moral teaching of Christ and the Church. Some teachers and writers have insisted that the best way to teach morality is to explain the Ten Commandments. Others have opted for a treatment of the "Beatitudes" as found in the Gospels. Still others have explained Catholic moral teaching under the banner of the great Christian virtues.

What I have tried to do is select several Scripture themes that are central to the following of Christ. I have then tried to *blend* a treatment of the Ten Commandments with a treatment of the great Christian virtues and have tried to show how the Church applies these to some of the pressing moral problems of our day.

Part One treats of *the foundations* of the moral teaching of Christ and the Church. Here the great virtue of charity or love is emphasized, for the Christian moral life is above all a life of love: God's love for us in Christ, and our loving response. Sin is considered, in effect, as a negative response to God's love. Finally, there is a brief examination of moral freedom and the dignity of moral conscience.

Part Two treats of our relationship *with God*. It touches on the first three commandments of the Decalogue and strives to highlight the virtues of faith, hope, and religion.

Part Three treats of our relationship *with other people*. It touches on the fourth to the tenth commandments. It focuses on the virtues of justice, piety, chastity, and honesty and how these virtues pertain to some of the urgent moral issues of our day.

I owe a debt of gratitude to many people who have helped me with this book. I thank Christopher Farrell, C.SS.R., and Roger Marchand for their overall editorial assistance. I thank my Redemptorist confreres: Richard Boever, Norman Muckerman, and David Polek — for reading the manuscript and giving me many helpful suggestions. Unfortunately, I alone am responsible for the defects of this book.

My purpose in writing this book was to shed light. I have tried to shed the light of Catholic teaching on the moral dimension of our lives. It will be enough for me if some of the light shines through!

Daniel L. Lowery, C.SS.R.

PART ONE:
THE FOUNDATIONS
OF FOLLOWING CHRIST

"Teacher, which commandment of the law is greatest?" Jesus said to him: "You shall love the Lord your God with your whole heart, with your whole soul, and with all your mind.' This is the greatest and first commandment. The second is like it: 'You shall love your neighbor as yourself.' On these two commandments the whole law is based, and the prophets as well."

— Matthew 22:36-40

Every Christian vocation is a vocation to love.

— Pope John Paul II

Sin is a spirit of selfishness rooted in our hearts and wills which wages war against God's plan for our fulfillment.

— American Bishops

Of itself conscience is a candle without a flame, but Christ the Light shines forth with his brightness and warmth from it.

— Bernard Häring, C.SS.R.

Christianity is not that mass of restrictions which the unbeliever imagines; on the contrary, it is peace, joy, life and love which, like the unseen throbbing of nature in early spring, is ever being renewed.

— Pope John XXIII

9

CHAPTER ONE
THE MANY FACES OF LOVE

Our God Who Calls

Because our minds are finite and because God is infinite, we can never know everything about God's dealing with us, his people. Yet some things, precious and powerful things, we do know. We know them because God has graciously revealed them to us. Vatican Council II reminds us: "By divine revelation God wished to manifest and communicate both himself and the eternal decrees of his will concerning the salvation of mankind" (*Divine Revelation*, 6). God's word is revealed to us especially in the Bible, in both the Old and New Testament.

As we meditate on God's revealed word — that word which like the boundless ocean has no limits — we begin to see that our God can, in a special way, be named *The God Who Calls*. Though all-powerful, God does not *force* his people. Always he respects our priceless gift of freedom. Yet he does call and invite. What is even more remarkable, he calls not merely in a general fashion but, like a concerned parent, he calls us each by name. "But now, thus says the LORD, who created you, O Jacob, and formed you, O Israel: Fear not, for I have redeemed you; I have called you by name: you are mine" (Isaiah 43:1).

The Bible is full of examples of God calling his people by name to be his disciples, his followers, his prophets, his witnesses in the world. In the first book of the Old Testament, we hear God calling Abraham, telling him to leave his country and his father's house and to take up the role God has prepared for him (Genesis 12:1). God surprises young Samuel by calling him by name and making him his witness (1 Samuel 3:10). In the moving scene of the Annunciation, God's messenger, the angel Gabriel, calls Mary to play a key role in salvation history (Luke 1:28). Jesus calls Matthew, the tax collector, to be his disciple (Matthew 9:9). And so it goes: God calling, calling.

God calls us, each by name, to be his followers. He does this especially through Baptism, the sacred sign by which Christ calls us to be his followers. The Church expresses this very beautifully in one of the prayers for the Christian initiation of adults: "Lord, you call these chosen ones to the glory of new birth in Christ . . . ." God calls us to nothing less than life in Christ!

The Good News is that Jesus Christ is our Savior and that we have life through him. "Yes, God so loved the world that he gave his only Son, that whoever believes in him may not die but may have eternal life. God did not send the Son into the world to condemn the world, but that the world might be saved through him" (John 3:16-17). And Jesus says of himself: ". . . I came that they might have life and have it to the full" (John 10:10).

The life to which God calls us is *a life of love*. Pope John Paul II expresses it in one sentence: "Every Christian vocation is a vocation to love." The Christian life, like a precious diamond, has many facets. To be a Christian means to be just and truthful and chaste and honest. But over and above everything else, we are called to love. This message fairly leaps from the pages of the Bible: "Hear, O Israel! The LORD is our God, the LORD alone! Therefore, you shall love the LORD, your God, with all your heart, and with all your soul, and with all your strength. Take to heart these words which I enjoin on you today. Drill them into your children. Speak of them at home and abroad, whether you are busy or at rest . . ." (Deuteronomy 6:4-7). And Jesus, in the celebrated response to the lawyer, says decisively: " '. . . love the Lord your God . . .' This is the greatest and first commandment. The second is like it: '. . . love your neighbor as yourself.' On these two commandments the whole law is based and the prophets as well" (Matthew 22:37-40).

If God calls us each by name to live a life of love, two questions logically come to mind. The first is, "What is meant by a life of love?" The chapters to follow are an attempt to answer that question. For the follower of Christ, a life of love does indeed mean many things: keeping the commandments, living by the Beatitudes, pursuing the virtues, applying Gospel values to real situations. But all of these separate items are seen as falling under the umbrella of love.

The second question, "How does one respond to God's call?" is at the heart of Christian morality. The answer is basically up to us. Our response to God's call can be positive and joyful or fearful and hesitant or even selfish and negative. The answer must come from the depths of our hearts. But always, in all of our conscious behavior, we are in fact responding in one way or another to God.

Saint Paul reminds us that "God is faithful, and it was he who called you to fellowship with his Son, Jesus Christ our Lord" (1 Corinthians 1:9). The ultimate moral question is: Shall we in turn be faithful to God and to his plan for us?

God's Plan for Us

Like an intricate painting which begins with a few broad strokes, the Bible offers a two-sentence summary of God's plan for us: "Love the Lord your God . . . Love your neighbor as yourself!" This has been rightly called "the great law of love."

Yet this great law of love, beautiful as it is, remains rather general. Does God's law contain any practical norms and concrete directions for us? The answer is yes. The Scriptures give not only the broad strokes but some of the intricate detail as well.

There is one very basic way in which God has shown us how the great law of love applies to the many dimensions of human life: namely, the *Decalogue,* commonly referred to as the Ten Commandments.

The story is an interesting one. It is told in the Book of Exodus, chapters 19 through 40. Here is an outline of the story. In the third month after the Israelites had left Egypt for the Promised Land, they arrived near Mount Sinai. God called Moses, the leader of the Israelites, and told him that he himself would appear to the people.

Two days later, thunder roared and lightning flashed and a trumpet's blast pierced the sky. Moses led the Israelites to the foot of the mountain. As the mountain shook, God spoke from the clouds. But the people, caught up in great fear and confusion, begged Moses to ask God *not* to speak to them.

Moses then went alone to talk to God. God gave him two tablets of stone on which were carved ten basic commandments or laws, visible messages from God to his people. On coming down from the mountain, however, Moses found the fickle Israelites adoring a golden calf made from their jewelry. In anger and disappointment, Moses flung down the tablets of stone and broke them.

Later, God told Moses to make two new tablets with the commandments engraved on them. These precious tablets were eventually placed in the Ark of the Covenant which rested in the Tabernacle. When Solomon built the magnificent Temple of Jerusalem, the Ark was placed in the innermost section called the "Holy of Holies."

But what were the commandments? Most of us have heard them, and many of us have memorized them, from childhood. They are spelled out in chapter 20 of the Book of Exodus. It is customary, in listing the Ten Commandments, to eliminate some of the detailed "explanation" as given in the Scripture texts. In line with this approach, the Ten Commandments may be stated as follows.

I, the Lord, am your God . . .
    You shall not have other gods besides me . . .
You shall not take the name of the Lord,
    your God, in vain . . .
Remember to keep holy the sabbath day . . .
Honor your father and mother . . .
You shall not kill.
You shall not commit adultery.
You shall not steal.
You shall not bear false witness against your neighbor.
You shall not covet your neighbor's wife . . .
You shall not covet your neighbor's house . . . .

It is evident that these commandments touch on some of the most basic human relationships. They are obviously not merely laws of good order or rules of good sportsmanship, like the laws governing fishing licenses or the rules applying to football. In the Judaeo-Christian tradition they have held an honored place.

Saint Augustine described the Ten Commandments as "messages from God." Saint Alphonsus Liguori called them "expressions of God's will." Pope John XXIII referred to them as "timeless guidelines for living.'' In a nutshell: they come from God who created us, who calls us by name, who knows our human nature, who loves us with an enduring love. Far from frustrating our human nature, the commandments show us how to fulfill ourselves, how to become more completely human.

The Ten Commandments touch upon our most basic relationships. Because we are *created* human beings, we must acknowledge our dependence on God, our Creator. We must, therefore, praise God, worship him alone, show reverence for his name. And because every other human person is, like us, loved by God, we must love and respect our neighbor in his or her life, family, property, and reputation. In brief, these commandments indicate how we are to live as human persons made in the image and likeness of God, how we are to relate both to God and to our fellow human beings.

Over the centuries there has been a running argument about the best way to present Christian morality. Some people feel that the approach of the Ten Commandments is too negative and legalistic. It seems not to be in accord with the great law of love. While it is undoubtedly true that the moral teaching of the Ten Commandments must be ''fleshed out'' by the moral teaching of Jesus, there is no need to eliminate them from a Christian view of morality. The most helpful approach — and it is the approach of this book — is that of Jesus himself. While it is true that Jesus went *beyond* the commandments in his teaching, it is also true that he *began* with them. Properly understood, the commandments help us fulfill the great law of love.

The Moral Teaching of Jesus

From what has already been said in these pages, certain questions naturally arise: What did Jesus say about the Ten Commandments? What did he add to these commandments?

First of all, Jesus made it clear that his teaching was not meant to reject the old law but, rather, to perfect it. He insisted that even the least of the commandments should be kept by his disciples. His ongoing battle with the Pharisees was not about the value of the commandments but about their hypocritical and nit-picking attitude toward the externals of the law.

''Do not think that I have come to abolish the law and the prophets. I have come, not to abolish them, but to fulfill them. Of this much I assure you: until heaven and earth pass away, not the smallest letter of the law, not the smallest part of a letter, shall be done away with until it all comes true. That is why whoever breaks the least significant of these commands and teaches others to do so shall be called least in the kingdom of God. Whoever fulfills and teaches these commands shall be great in the kingdom of God'' (Matthew 5:17-19).

On several occasions, moreover, Jesus repeated the Ten Commandments and urged their observance. One such occasion was his meeting with "the rich young man," as he has come to be known in history. Saint Matthew's Gospel describes the scene in these words: "Another time a man came up to him and said, 'Teacher, what good must I do to possess everlasting life?' He answered, 'Why do you question me about what is good? There is One who is good. If you wish to enter into life, keep the commandments.' 'Which ones?' he asked. Jesus replied, ' "You shall not kill"; "You shall not commit adultery"; "You shall not steal"; "You shall not bear false witness"; "Honor your father and your mother"; and "Love your neighbor as yourself." ' The young man said to him, 'I have kept all these; what do I need to do further?' Jesus told him, 'If you seek perfection, go, sell your possessions, and give to the poor. You will then have treasure in heaven. Afterward, come back and follow me' '' (Matthew 19:16-21).

This passage points out several elements of the teaching of Jesus. It is clear that the follower of Jesus must hold the commandments in the highest regard. They are, as it were, the *starting point* of our following of Jesus. It is also clear that Jesus goes beyond these basic commandments and calls this young man to a life of poverty and detachment, a call which he found too difficult to accept.

In the famous "Sermon on the Mount" Jesus both demands the observance of the commandments and goes beyond them. (It is most instructive to read the entire Sermon with this thought in mind. It is found in chapters 5, 6, and 7 of the Gospel of Matthew.) Here we will look at a few examples from the teaching of Jesus to illustrate the basic point.

Let us take the example of murder. "You have heard the commandment imposed on your forefathers, 'You shall not commit murder' . . . What I say to you is: everyone who grows angry with his brother shall be liable to judgment; any man who uses abusive language toward his brother shall be answerable to the Sanhedrin, and if he holds him in contempt he risks the fires of Gehenna'' (Matthew 5:21-23).

In this example we see how Jesus demands the keeping of the basic commandment and more besides. It is as if Jesus were saying, "If you want to be my follower, you must not commit murder. But you can't stop there. You must avoid anger. But you can't stop there; you must avoid abusive language. But you can't stop there; you must not hold others in contempt . . . ." This is the pattern he follows in teaching about the other commandments as well.

There is, however, one very special commandment that Jesus gave to his followers, and this one seems to go far beyond the old law. It is the commandment to love even our enemies. "You have heard the commandment, 'You shall love your countryman but hate your enemy.' My command to you is: love your enemies, pray for your persecutors" (Matthew 5:43-44). This commandment, opposed to all "commonsense" views of morality, is distinctive of the teaching of Jesus. It is perhaps the most demanding moral norm he ever gave us.

Yet another dimension of the moral teaching of Jesus may be equally demanding, though not as measurable. In stark contrast to the morality of the Pharisees, Jesus taught *a morality of the heart*. As sparkling water emerges from deep springs, so true morality arises from the mind and will and heart. Jesus was more concerned with interior dispositions than he was with external actions. ". . . Give ear and try to understand. It is not what goes into a man's mouth that makes him impure; it is what comes out of his mouth . . . From the mind stem evil designs — murder, adulterous conduct, fornication, stealing, false witness, blasphemy. These are the things that make a man impure" (Matthew 15:10-20).

To Jesus the internal motive, "the heart," is of primary importance. External actions obviously have their own importance, but their real morality must be judged according to the motivation from which they spring. Those who "do the right thing" but for wrong motives (such as human respect, public reputation) have not yet internalized the moral teaching of Jesus.

In truth, internalizing the moral teaching of Jesus is a lifelong task. A key element in that task is how we think about God.

God's Great Love for Us

The way we think about God, the image we have of him, is extremely important in living a Christian life. If we think about God in a negative way, as one who really doesn't love us but rather keeps constant tabs on us and is ever ready to punish us for our mistakes and sins, then our response to him will be joyless and minimal. If we believe that God's love and goodness are dependent on our own good actions, then we will easily doubt his love and goodness.

It is hard to think of anything more important for us than to grasp and appreciate how much God loves us. The awareness of God's love warms us when our hearts are cold and dreary, strengthens us when we are weak and wavering, holds us up when we feel like falling down. We cannot be faithful followers of Jesus without experiencing God's love for us. When we do experience it, we can be saints!

When we speak of God and his love, we speak of marvelous mysteries. While it is beyond our capacities to understand everything about God, there are some things we can understand, because he has revealed them to us. We can understand something about *the qualities of God's love.*

First of all, *God's love for us is gratuitous or free.* As if by a kind of spiritual osmosis, we sometimes receive the impression that God loves us *because* we perform good deeds or because we live a good moral life. The Scriptures clearly proclaim that such is not the case. "But when the kindness and love of God our Savior appeared, he saved us; not because of any righteous deed we had done, but because of his mercy . . ." (Titus 3:4-5). Similarly, in the first letter of John we read: "God's love was revealed in our midst in this way: he sent his only Son to the world that we might have life through him. Love, then, consists in this: not that we have loved God but that he has loved us and has sent his Son as an offering for our sins" (1 John 4:9-10). God's love, in other words, is a free gift.

Secondly, *God's love for us is unconditional.* Conditional love is partial love. It subtly implies that you are loved *because* you are smart or beautiful or humorous. Naturally you wonder, "But will I be loved if I become stupid or ugly or grumpy?" There are no conditions on God's love for us. Nothing can make God stop loving us, not even sin.

Father John Powell, S.J., expresses in human terms God's unconditional love for us: "I want to love you. That is all. I just want to love you. If you choose to leave me, I will not stop you. I will leave you free, but I will always love you. There may be a time when you will put something between our love for each other. There may be that time in your life when you will separate yourself from my love, but never believe that you have lost my love. You can only refuse, but you can never lose my love" *(Free to Be Me)*.

Thirdly, *God's love for us is everlasting*. In a tender analogy, the Scripture compares God's love for us with the love of a mother for her child. "Can a mother forget her infant, be without tenderness for the child of her womb? Even should she forget, I will never forget you" (Isaiah 49:15). With majestic eloquence Saint Paul, who experienced the love of God so deeply, writes: "I am certain that neither death nor life, neither angels nor principalities, neither the present nor the future, nor powers, neither height nor depth nor any other creature, will be able to separate us from the love of God that comes to us in Christ Jesus, our Lord" (Romans 8:38-39).

Just as a negative image of God can make us fearful and discouraged in living a Christian life, so a positive acceptance of God's free, unconditional, and everlasting love for us can make us eager and generous in striving to live a life of love in return. When we begin to see our moral efforts precisely as *responses* to God's love, we are on the road to true Christian holiness. This theme is captured beautifully in *Faith* by Louise Morgan Sili:

> All we know is trust
> And trust is born of love, and love of
>   God,
> And we were given what we call our
>   reason
> In order thus to reason back to love;
> For all the child knows is the love he
>   feels
> For those who gave him being, and all
>   man knows
> Is that God gave him being, and Him
>   he loves,
> And reverences, and forever seeks,
>   His Father, and his God.

A practical conclusion from this reflection is that whenever we examine our conscience or review our moral life, we should *start* with a prayer of thanks to God for his great love. Only in light of that love should we look at our sinfulness. That's the way it should be, for "God has saved us and has called us to a holy life, not because of any merit of ours but according to his own design — the grace held out to us in Christ Jesus before the world began . . ." (2 Timothy 1:9).

Love One Another

The centerpiece of the moral teaching of Jesus is what he calls "his own" commandment: "This is my commandment: love one another as I have loved you . . . . The command I give you is this, that you love one another" (John 15:12,17). Because the word "love" is used so frequently and in so many different ways, we can easily become confused about it. Though Jesus did not write a neat treatise on the kind of love he was talking about, he did indicate some of the qualities it should possess.

Jesus presents himself as not only a teacher of love but even more as an example. In the powerful symbol of washing the feet of his disciples, Jesus shows how real and practical and humble love must be. "Do you understand what I just did for you? You address me as 'Teacher' and 'Lord,' and fittingly enough, for that is what I am. But if I washed your feet — I who am Teacher and Lord — then you must wash each other's feet" (John 13:12-14). Jesus gives an example of sincere concern and practical service.

On the Cross Jesus gives an even more tremendous example of love. "There is no greater love than this: to lay down one's life for one's friends" (John 15:13). In his sacrifice of himself, that is precisely what Jesus did. The early Christians did not miss the lesson. "The way we came to understand love was that he laid down his life for us; we too must lay down our lives for our brothers" (1 John 3:16). The love to which Jesus calls his followers is demanding, calling for self-sacrifice, at times even (in the phrase made popular by Dorothy Day) "a harsh and dreadful thing."

The love which Jesus taught is universal in its scope, all-embracing, "for all." "See that no one returns evil to any other; always seek one another's good and, for that matter, the good of all" (1 Thessalonians 5: Vatican Council II expresses it this way: "Christian charity truly extends to all, without distinction of race, social condition or religion. It looks for neither gain nor gratitude" *(The Church's Missionary Activity,* 12). A constant temptation for the Christian is to draw lines in the practice of charity: racial lines, religious lines, personality lines. The love to which we are called by Christ, however, allows us to draw no lines whatever. In the words of Saint Paul, "There does not exist among you Jew or Greek, slave or freeman, male or female. All are one in Christ Jesus" (Galatians 3:28).

It has been rightly said that "they do not love that do not show their love." Christian love is characterized, therefore, not by vague and "dreamy" affection but by concrete acts of service and concern. Love must prove itself in the ordinary relationships of daily life: in the family, at work, at school, in the neighborhood. A common moral pitfall is to think of love in large and dramatic terms. "If this would happen, then I would . . . ." But such dramatic moments, as experience testifies, do not come often in our lives. Far more frequent are the day-by-day demands of love. Perhaps that is why Saint Paul in his great hymn to love speaks of the nitty-gritty virtues: "Love is patient; love is kind. Love is not jealous, it does not put on airs, it is not snobbish. Love is never rude, it is not self-seeking, it is not prone to anger; neither does it brood over injuries" (1 Corinthians 13:4-5).

The other side of the coin of love is hatred. John minces no words about hatred: "Anyone who hates his brother is a murderer, and you know that eternal life abides in no murderer's heart" (1 John 3:15). Hatred breeds a large family. The "eldest child" is a spirit of unforgiveness. If there is anything clear in the teaching of Jesus, it is that we can expect God's forgiveness of our sins *only if* we are willing to forgive others. "If you forgive the faults of others, your heavenly Father will forgive you yours. If you do not forgive others, neither will your Father forgive you" (Matthew 6:14-15). It is as simple as that — and as difficult.

The spirit of unforgiveness tends to express itself in the form of grudges or resentments. Who can count the ways in which these resentments show themselves? Some of the usual ways are: one person refusing to speak to another for long periods of time (even in the same family); sarcastic or hurtful remarks "to get even"; one person constructing a martyr complex that is impervious to all outside influences — and many others. Unforgiving and resentful people are hard to live with. Their spirit infects everyone around them. But it also infects *them*. Resentments are like cancers of the soul. They fester and eat away at one's happiness and peace of mind. Psychologists know that if these resentments are allowed to go untended, they eventually squeeze their way out in the form of alcoholism, drug addiction, destructive sex, and the like. Almost every self-help group insists that the individual start dealing with resentments as a first step toward better mental and emotional health.

A news item that was broadcast many years ago has always stayed in my mind. It was right after the Second World War; an interviewer was speaking to Madame Chiang Kai-shek. At that sad hour she was able to say, "No matter what we have suffered, we must try to forgive those who have injured us . . . Christ taught us to hate evil in men, but not men themselves." That is the challenge that faces every Christian!

Saint Paul had a way of summarizing basic themes of the Gospel. And so he wrote: "Love never wrongs the neighbor, hence love is the fulfillment of the law" (Romans 13:10).

True Love of Self

On many occasions, as we have seen, Jesus firmly repeated the twofold commandment of the Old Testament concerning love of God and love of neighbor. One such occasion was in response to a lawyer who asked him a question "in an attempt to trip him up." The question was, " 'Teacher, which commandment of the law is the greatest?' Jesus said to him: ' "You shall love the Lord your God with your whole heart, with your whole soul, and with all your mind." This is the greatest and first commandment. The second is like it: "You shall love your neighbor as yourself." On these two commandments the whole law is based, and the prophets as well' " (Matthew 22:36-40).

How many commandments do we have in this saying of Jesus? This may seem like a strange question, since Jesus himself says that there are *two* commandments. Yet it is possible to say that there are actually *three* commandments. One of them is a "hidden" commandment, in the sense that Jesus does not spell it out. Yet he seems to assume that it will be observed. It is almost as if he takes it for granted. What I am referring to is the "as yourself" of the statement of Jesus. "You shall love your neighbor *as yourself.*"

What does this "as yourself" mean? In my opinion, it means that the norm or measure for loving our neighbor is taken from the way in which we love ourselves. Or, to put it negatively: If we do not love ourselves, we will not be able to love our neighbor, and so we will not be able to fulfill the second commandment of Jesus. A true love of self seems necessary, therefore, to live a Christian moral life.

Do you think that most people love themselves? We could probably have a very lively discussion about this question. My conviction is that many people do *not* love themselves. And many experts in the fields of psychology and human relations are also of this opinion. Many people, the evidence seems to show, suffer from a poor self-image, low self-esteem, and a lack of self-worth. In some people there is present even self-hatred or self-loathing.

A reader may be tempted to object to this line of thought. The real problem in the world today, he or she may feel, is precisely *too much self-love,* too much selfishness, too much concern for Number One. Without doubt, selfishness is rampant in our world. It is the root of all sin. It manifests itself in a hundred different ways.

We must be careful, however, to make a distinction between selfishness and true self-love. They are not the same thing. True self-love means that a person believes and accepts a profound truth about himself or herself: namely, that he or she is made in the image and likeness of God, is profoundly loved by God and lavishly gifted by God. The psalmist speaks of the human person as the jewel of creation. "What is man that you should be mindful of him, or the son of man that you should care for him? You have made him little less than the angels, and crowned him with glory and honor" (Psalm 8:5-6).

A poor self-image results from the feedback we receive from others. One theory of social psychology is called "the looking glass self," because it implies that we get our self-image from the reflection of other people. If important people in our lives (such as parents, teachers, peers) send us mostly negative feedback, we quite naturally begin to see ourselves in this way. If others imply that we are evil or ugly or worthless, we gradually begin to believe that we are so.

Father John Powell, S.J., explains this point well: "I don't know how it all got started, but somehow we were brought up on the tradition that we had to dislike ourselves. The appropriate response to ourselves was to be dissatisfied and to try harder. And that is toxic. That is destructive. That is shriveling and constricting. If you think of yourself as inadequate, that's the person you will act out and communicate" *(Free to Be Me)*.

In line with this: Is not much of our anger, for example, aimed at ourselves rather than at others? Don't some young people reject their faith in God or at least their practice of it in order to "get even" with the adult "authority figures" who have hurt them? Isn't the abuse of alcohol and drugs often enough traceable to self-hatred? How much of the hard-core sexual exploitation of our society is due in reality to self-loathing?

Unfortunately, there are no quick and easy solutions to our lack of self-love. Yet, from the viewpoint of faith, there are certain starting points that can help us. It seems most important for us to make our own the most basic faith conviction of all: namely, God loves me, has always loved me, will always love me! Earlier in this chapter we tried to focus on the truth that God's love for us is free and unconditional. If we can believe that, we will begin to love ourselves, not for false reasons but for the best of all reasons!

The Gospels show Jesus freeing countless people from demons of every type and description. The demon of self-hatred is one that prowls our world today. In my mind's eye, I see Jesus moving among us by his power and grace and freeing us from the demons that keep us from loving ourselves and that keep us, therefore, from loving others.

CHAPTER TWO
THE MANY FACES OF SIN

Sin: Original and Personal

With his customary insight Thomas Merton wrote about "the moral theology of the devil." Not surprisingly, the devil's moral theology has a lot to say about sin! Part of the devil's strategy is so to confuse the notion of sin as to make people downplay it or explain it away. Another part of the strategy, however, is to make sin seem so trivial and irrelevant as to be unworthy of the attention of serious men and women.

Without cynicism, and at the risk of oversimplification, it is possible to feel that Catholic moral theology has not always completely escaped these dangers. Theologians who deal with the concept of sin at a very deep level sometimes seem to make it so esoteric that the average person is incapable of understanding it, let alone committing it. Catechists and teachers, on the other hand, in an admirable effort to communicate something about the reality of sin, especially to young people, run the risk of "dummying it down" so much that almost every evil act is a "mortal sin." The sad result may be that people, as they mature, tend to disregard the very idea of sin.

Sin has many faces and wears many masks as well. It is helpful from time to time to sit back and reflect on basic Catholic teaching about sin, especially in relationship to our fundamental vocation to live a life of love. An important starting point for reflection is the distinction between original sin and personal sin.

The Second Vatican Council states: "Although set by God in a state of rectitude, man, enticed by the evil one, abused his freedom at the very start of history. He lifted himself against God and sought to attain his goal apart from him" (*Church in the Modern World*, 13). This is a concise description of original sin, the sin that occurred at the *origins* of the human race.

The Book of Genesis tells the story of that original sin in striking detail. The first two chapters of Genesis tell how God created all things, including man and woman, and saw that they were "very good." In chapter 3, however, Adam rejects God and separates himself from him. Adam tries to hide from God, blames Eve for his sin, experiences the pangs of guilt.

From this original sin of Adam, a host of evils came into the world. Chapters 4 through 11 of Genesis describe in narrative form how the first sin brought a mushroom cloud of evil into the world. Cain murders his brother Abel in cold blood. Sin is so rampant that God sends a great flood (from which only Noah and his family are preserved), the flood that highlights the chaos and destruction brought by sin into the beauty of creation.

Even this does not open the eyes of the people. In chapter 11 of Genesis we see human beings still defying God and wanting to be his equal by building a tower that would reach to the heavens. The Tower of Babel speaks eloquently about the effects of sin: human beings not only reject God but also reject and despise one another. There is now division and hatred among nations.

"According to Genesis, a world of beauty was deformed by sin. The ongoing result has been division, pain, bloodshed, loneliness and death. This tragic narrative has a familiar feel to it. The reality it points to is a basic part of human experience. It is no surprise that this reality — the fact of original sin and its effect in us all — is a teaching of the Church" (*Handbook for Today's Catholic*, 28).

According to Catholic teaching, every mortal born into the world (with the exception of the Virgin Mary, who was immaculately conceived) is affected by original sin. This is not a personal sin actually committed by each individual, but rather, in the words of Pope Paul VI, "It is human nature so fallen, stripped of the grace that clothed it, injured in its own natural powers and subjected to the dominion of death, that is transmitted to all men, and it is in this sense that every man is born in sin" *(Credo of the People of God)*. Original sin means, therefore, that each "descendant of Adam" is created without sanctifying grace and is subject to concupiscence (the inclination to sin) as well as the punishment of death. Sin came into the world through one man and death through sin, and so death spread to all men because all men sinned (see Romans 5:12).

Yet at the same time the Church rejects the idea that human nature as such is corrupt. Weak and inconstant, yes, but not completely incapable of good acts or free choices. Above all, fallen human nature is capable of receiving sanctifying grace ("new life") through the death and Resurrection of Christ. ". . . For if by the offense of one man all died, much more did the grace of God and the gracious gift of the one man, Jesus Christ, abound for all" (Romans 5:15). This grace of God, this new life in Christ, is passed on to us through the sacrament of Baptism. Thus the darkness of original sin is overcome by the bright victory of Christ over sin and death.

Personal sin is not the same as original sin. While original sin is the state of alienation from God into which all human beings are born, personal sin is a fundamental choice against God, a free and willing turning away from his love. It goes without saying that the full reality of sin cannot be captured in one definition. Over the centuries sin has been described in a number of ways: for example, as "a turning away from God," "an offense against God," "a free transgression of the law of God," "a failure to love God and others."

The American bishops have summarized a great deal of Christian tradition in their clear statement about sin: "We must recognize the brutal reality of sin. It is different from unavoidable failure or limitation. We all fail often through no fault of our own, and we all experience human limitations, among which the ultimate limitation is death. It is a sign of maturity to be able to accept our limitations and discover meaning in our failures.

"Sin is different. It is a spirit of selfishness rooted in our hearts and wills which wages war against God's plan for our fulfillment. It is a rejection, either partial or total, of one's role as a child of God and a member of his people, a rejection of the spirit of sonship, love and life. We sin first in our hearts, although our sins are expressed in outward acts and their consequences" (*To Live in Christ Jesus*, 5).

This compact statement indicates some of the most profound truths about sin. First of all, sin is essentially in the *free will* of the human person; it is a fundamental choice. Sin is not primarily in the *act* (for example, theft, adultery, lying), though the choice is commonly expressed through an act. There are, however, sins which are not expressed in external action; these "internal" sins include rash judgments, lustful desires, approval of past evil actions, and the like. Jesus speaks of an internal sin when he says that "anyone who looks lustfully at a woman has already committed adultery with her in his thoughts" (Matthew 5:28) and when he admonishes, "If you want to avoid judgment, stop passing judgment" (Matthew 7:1).

Furthermore, as we know from experience, we can sin not only by doing something which should not be done but also by failing to do what ought to be done! "Sins of omission," as they are commonly called, are for many people their most frequent sins. For example, I know that my neighbor is confined to bed and in need of someone to shop for her, but I make sure it isn't I! There is a strong temptation in such cases to let things pass, not to make an effort. Bernard Häring, C.SS.R., wisely remarks: "Perhaps the sins which consist in the commission of evil do not constitute as grave a peril for the kindom of God as the more numerous sins of neglect of the good which must be done" *(The Law of Christ)*.

Having looked at the distinction between original sin and personal sin, we are now in a position to review a further distinction between mortal sin and venial sin.

Sin: Mortal and Venial

Personal sin is traditionally divided into *mortal* (serious, grave) sin and *venial* (light, "easily forgiven") sin. Saint Thomas throws light on the distinction: "The division into mortal and venial sins is not like the division of a genus into two species; they are not specifically different kinds of sin, determined by the objects to which they turn. The difference between mortal and venial sin is decided by the stage reached by the disordered turning away from God . . . When our acts are so deranged that we turn away from our last end, namely God, to whom we should be united by charity, then the sin is mortal. Short of that, the sin is venial."

The "disordered turning away from God" emphasizes once again that sin is primarily in the will. Modern theologians often refer to mortal sin as a *fundamental option* or *basic choice*.

Anthony Wilhelm says that "mortal sin, then, is a fundamental choice of ourself over God that engages us to the depths of our being" (*Christ Among Us*). Timothy O'Connell writes that "mortal sin as an act is nothing else than a synonym for fundamental option. A mortal sin . . . is that act by which we substantially reject God and assume instead a posture apart from and in alienation from God" (*Principles for a Catholic Morality*).

These and many other theologians are trying to stress how basic, how profound, how deliberate a mortal sin really is. Mortal sins do not happen "out of the blue" or "by accident." Mortal sin arises from the depths of the personality and involves a fundamental attitude toward God or people. This important emphasis has led some theologians to assert that a mortal sin cannot be committed in any single act. This seems to be an unnecessary exaggeration. The Congregation for the Doctrine of the Faith strikes a balanced note when it states: "In reality, it is precisely the fundamental option which in the last resort defines a person's moral disposition. But it can be completely changed by particular acts, especially when, as often happens, these have been prepared for by previous more superficial acts" (*Declaration on Sexual Ethics,* 10).

Whatever particular definition or description one gives to mortal sin, the reality of it has always been considered the greatest evil in the universe — greater than poverty, sickness, war, death. Because it is such a great evil, there has developed over the centuries a practical way of trying to discern when a mortal sin is committed. These are the so-called *conditions* of mortal sin. Before a person is guilty of mortal sin, three conditions must be verified: (1) the matter must be grave or serious; (2) there must be sufficient reflection; (3) there must be full consent of the will. A brief review of these may be helpful.

The matter must be grave or serious. If we think of our ordinary human relationships, we readily see that there are certain kinds of actions which place only a slight strain on the relationship, while there are others that tend to *destroy* the relationship. If a person makes a slightly insulting remark to a friend, that remark may occasion a certain temporary coolness in the friendship, but would not ordinarily break the bond of friendship. If, however, a person were to violate a basic right of his or her friend or commit an abusive act against him or her, we would expect that the friendship would come to an end.

In a similar way, the Scriptures and the teaching of the Church point out that certain kinds of human actions are of greater moral significance than others. They are the kinds of actions that bring about notable harm in our relationship with God and with others. They are the kinds of actions that engage us in a serious way.

Saint Paul, on a number of occasions, contrasts the works of the flesh and the works of the spirit. He does not hesitate to spell out the kinds of actions he is talking about in these categories of "flesh" (evil, sin) and "spirit" (virtue). "Can you not realize that the unholy will not fall heir to the kingdom of God? Do not deceive yourselves: no fornicators, idolaters, or adulterers, no sodomites, thieves, misers, or drunkards, no slanderers or robbers will inherit God's kingdom" (1 Corinthians 6:9-10).

This list and other similar lists (see Galatians 5:19-21) are not meant to be exhaustive. Over the centuries, as new moral problems have arisen, the Church and its theologians have addressed themselves to other kinds of actions that involve "serious matter." Thus, Vatican Council II condemned as a crime "every act of war directed to the indiscriminate destruction of whole cities or vast areas with their inhabitants"; Pope Paul VI certainly included artificial contraception under serious matter; the American bishops argued that racial discrimination is a destructive evil. And so on.

One aspect of this problem that has caused considerable misunderstanding and dispute is the role of conscience in deciding what is right and wrong. We will return to this question when we treat of conscience. If my conscience says that adultery is right and yours says it is wrong, where do we stand? The Second Vatican Council said: "In the formation of their consciences, the Christian faithful ought carefully to attend to the sacred and certain doctrine of the Church" (*Religious Freedom*, 14). The American bishops have expressed it this way: "Where are we to look for the teachings of Jesus, hear his voice and discern his will? In Scripture, whose books were written under the inspiration of the Holy Spirit. In prayer, where we grow in knowledge and love of Christ and in commitment to his service. In the events of human life and history, where Christ and his Spirit are at work. In the Church, where all these things converge" (*To Live in Christ Jesus*, 10).

Secondly, *for mortal sin there must be sufficient reflection*. This "sufficient reflection" is sometimes called *full advertence*. It implies that a person is clearly aware of the seriousness of the action he or she is contemplating and the choice he or she is making. This knowledge or advertence implies the ability to *evaluate* and *appreciate* moral values. It is, as it were, "knowledge with a twist." It demands a certain insight into moral values such as love, justice, honesty, truth.

In this context, many pastors and religious educators doubt that a child is capable of committing a mortal sin. The child may have reached "the use of reason" but ordinarily would not have the kind of appreciation of moral values necessary for sin. This does not mean that a child is unable to do wrong acts. A child may, for example, steal a precious diamond ring. But does the child have any real appreciation of why stealing is wrong, why the private property of others is worthy of respect, why a diamond ring is so valuable to the owner?

Moreover, moral maturity does not necessarily go along with physical maturity. There are teenagers, and indeed adults, who seem to suffer from a stunted moral growth. The lack of moral education and value clarification in many homes and schools often has the effect of rendering people incapable of appreciating moral values. The challenge of moral education is surely one of the greatest facing modern societies.

Thirdly, *there must be full consent of the will*. Without doubt this is the most important condition for mortal sin. Sin is essentially a free choice, an act of the free will. Without freedom, there cannot be guilt or moral responsibility in the proper sense of the word. Full consent of the will means that a person freely chooses to do what he or she knows is seriously evil even though he or she could stop from doing it.

The exercise of freedom can be limited by many influences, such as drugs, overpowering emotions, external force. In the next chapter we will look briefly at some of the influences that either destroy or diminish the exercise of free will. Some people react very negatively to the mention of limitations on freedom. In the legal forum the courts have struggled with the "innocent by reason of insanity" plea, as in the case of John Hinckley, who attempted to assassinate President Reagan in 1981. While this area of human life is obviously complicated, the point here is that if a person is not free, mortal sin is not possible.

These few reflections on the conditions for mortal sin should not lead us to think that these matters of sin, guilt, and responsibility are "crystal clear." As in many other areas of human life, it is easier to talk about these conditions than it is to apply them. There are many ambiguities in human behavior. Moral growth, like growth of any kind, takes time. While trying to avoid the modern mentality that wants to remove "sin" and "responsibility" from the dictionary, we should equally avoid the trap of casually categorizing mortal sins. We need balance, insight, and compassion in this very important area of Christian life.

Venial sin may be described as a less serious rejection of God's love. A venial sin is not a fundamental choice against God, not a complete turning away from him. Venial sin is a failure to love God and others as much as we should; it is a transient neglect of God and his law. Saint Thomas puts it this way: "Although a man who commits a venial sin does not actually refer his act to God, nevertheless he still keeps God as his habitual end. He does not decisively set himself on turning away from God, but from overfondness for a created good he falls short of God. He is like a man who loiters, but without leaving the way."

Traditionally, a sin is considered venial if the matter is not serious (for example, an angry word as compared to an act of violence); or, if serious, the person is not sufficiently aware of the evil involved or does not fully consent to the evil. Though venial sin does not destroy God's love in us, nor does it turn us away from God in a fundamental way, it does lessen our love for God and others, it does make us less fervent in our commitment to Christ, and it does tend to "soften us up" for mortal sin. The saints are practically unanimous in encouraging us to struggle against venial sin, so that the love of God can bloom and grow in us.

Sin and Reconciliation

John Cardinal Newman asserts that, in the Catholic tradition, it is better for the sun and moon to drop from the heavens and for the earth to fail than that one person should commit a deliberate sin. As with one voice, many of the saints said the same thing. Mortal sin is "the greatest evil in the universe."

Those of us who are not saints may sheepishly admit that we hardly ever think this way. The life we lead tends to be superficial and distracting. The inner meaning of sin is a faith conviction that grows only in the atmosphere of deep reflection and prayer.

Indeed, even in the best of circumstances, it is hard to understand "the mystery of iniquity."

According to Catholic teaching, *sin is a personal tragedy.* As we have seen, God's original plan was to share his own divine life with men and women. That plan was frustrated by original sin. But through Christ the plan was restored. "I came," Jesus said of himself, "that they might have life and have it to the full" (John 10:10). "God's love was revealed in our midst in this way: he sent his only Son to the world that we might have life through him" (1 John 4:9).

We share this new life through Baptism. "Are you not aware that we who were baptized into Christ Jesus were baptized into his death? Through baptism into his death we were buried with him, so that, just as Christ was raised from the dead by the glory of the Father, we too might live a new life" (Romans 6:3-4). Mortal means death-inflicting. Mortal sin inflicts death on this new life. That, in the truest sense of the word, is a tragedy.

In its most profound meaning, sin is a fundamental choice *against love.* But, as we saw earlier, we were made for love, called to live a life of love. "We have come to know and to believe in the love God has for us. God is love, and he who abides in love abides in God, and God in him" (1 John 4:16). It is love alone that can fulfill us, make us happy, bring us peace. Tragic is the choice that turns us away from that for which we were made!

The Church's teaching on hell points up the final tragedy of sin. In essence, hell means the loss of God. Hell has been called the house of hate. There is no love, no possibility of love. Thomas Merton says that hell is where no one has anything in common with anybody else except the fact that they all hate one another.

In addition to the personal dimension of sin, there is also a *social* or *community* dimension. For we are not merely individuals, we are members of the People of God, the Body of Christ. "God did not create man for life in isolation, but for the formation of social unity. So also 'it has pleased God to make men holy and save them not merely as individuals, without any mutual bonds, but by making them into a single people, a people which acknowledges him in truth and serves him in holiness.' So from the beginning of salvation history he has chosen men not just as individuals but as members of a certain community" (*Church in the Modern World*, 32).

Just as there is solidarity in holiness and salvation, so also there is solidarity in sin. If one member of the body is holy, to paraphrase Saint Paul, his or her holiness affects the whole body; if one member sins, the whole body is touched by that sin. The bond of unity in the Body of Christ needs the cooperative reinforcement of all the members. Dom Griffiths has expressed this well: "To be a Christian is to accept the responsibility for sin not only in oneself but in others also. It is to recognize that we all bear the responsibility for one another" *(The Golden String)*.

The term "social sin" is being used more and more these days to express the idea that sin exists in some of the structures of human communities. "Sinful structures are not simply imperfect human organizations; rather, such structures involve a systematic abuse of the rights of certain groups and individuals. The sinfulness lies in the unjust way in which social relationships are organized. An extreme example is institutionalized racial or ethnic segregation; a less striking example is the absence or inadequacy of minimum wage laws. A very contemporary example is the imbalance in the distribution of the world's goods which calls for a new international economic order" *(Sharing the Light of Faith,* 165).

Whether we consider sin on the personal or the social level, we see it as estrangement, alienation, brokenness, division. Into this desperate situation comes the call of Jesus: "Reform your lives! The kingdom of heaven is at hand" (Matthew 4:17). This call to conversion, this invitation to grace is the good news of the Gospel! All of our human relationships stand in need of reconciliation, of healing, of renewal.

In the name and spirit of Christ, the Church calls us to repentance and reconciliation. Jesus took on our human condition, suffered, died, and rose again to deliver us from the power of sin. "This means that if anyone is in Christ, he is a new creation. The old order has passed away; now all is new! . . . I mean that God, in Christ, was reconciling the world to himself, not counting men's transgressions against them, and that he has entrusted the message of reconciliation to us" (2 Corinthians 5:17,19).

This repentance and reconciliation is carried out in many different ways, especially in the liturgy "when the faithful confess that they are sinners and ask pardon of God and of their brothers and sisters. This happens in penitential services, in the proclamation of the word of God, in prayer, and in the penitential aspects of the eucharistic celebration'' (*Decree on Penance,* 1973, 4).

We engage in conversion and reconciliation in a special way through the sacrament of Penance (about which Pope Paul VI said, "We will accustom ourselves henceforth to define it as *the sacrament of reconciliation*"). This sacrament brings about reconciliation with God and with our brothers and sisters who are harmed by our sins. The rite of reconciliation, especially when its communal aspects are made visible, is indeed an eloquent call to renew all things in Christ. "In fact, men frequently join together to commit injustice. It is thus only fitting that they should help each other in doing penance so that they who are freed from sin by the grace of Christ may work with all men of good will for justice and peace in the world" (*Decree on Penance,* 5).

The sacrament of Penance, which seems to have lost its appeal for many Catholics today, is still one of the Church's most beautiful sacraments. It expresses the tender compassion and mercy of Christ which he extended to all who responded to his call for conversion. The power to forgive sins and to effect reconciliation is one of the greatest gifts of Christ to the Church, and one of the most needed.

The essence of this sacrament is stated thus: "The follower of Christ who has sinned but who has been moved by the Holy Spirit to come to the sacrament of Penance should above all be converted to God with his whole heart. This inner conversion of heart embraces sorrow for sin and the intent to lead a new life. It is expressed through confession made to the Church, due satisfaction, and amendment of life. God grants pardon of sin through the Church, which works by the ministry of priests" (*Decree on Penance,* 6).

According to this same decree, the fundamental norms governing the sacrament of Penance are as follows:

1. To obtain the saving remedy of the sacrament of Penance, according to the plan of our merciful God, the faithful must confess to a priest each and every grave sin which they remember upon examination of their conscience.

2. Frequent and careful celebration of this sacrament is also a very useful remedy for venial sin. This is not a mere ritual repetition or psychological exercise but a serious striving to perfect the grace of Baptism, so that, as we bear in our body the death of Jesus Christ, his life may be seen in us ever more clearly.

The Church encourages the celebration of this sacrament especially during the penitential season of Lent. The so-called "Easter duty" requires that a Catholic receive Holy Communion during the Easter season (in the United States the time for fulfilling this obligation extends from the first Sunday of Lent till Trinity Sunday). Strictly speaking, the obligation to receive the sacrament of Penance holds only if a person is conscious of unconfessed mortal sin. Yet the more frequent reception of this sacrament, especially in the more relational way in which the new rite is carried out, is of great help in living the Christian life and in seeking spiritual direction in one's life.

CHAPTER THREE
THE MANY FACES OF MORALITY

Freedom: Gift and Challenge

Saint Thomas Aquinas had a knack for making good distinctions. In his treatise on morality he made a particularly important distinction between *a human act* and *an act of man*. A human act is one which flows from the deliberate and free will of the human person, an act which is under the dominion and mastery of that person. For example, I sing a song, write a letter, crack a safe, tell a lie. An act of man, on the other hand, is an act which proceeds from some impulse of nature but without deliberation and freedom; for example, I blink, I cough, I dream.

What Saint Thomas was concerned about was that we understand what *human* means. "Only those acts which are under the dominion or mastery of man are really human. What makes man master of his acts is his reason and will. Therefore human acts are those which proceed from the reason and free will of man." He was also concerned that we understand what *moral* means. "Only the human act can be called a moral act, that is, an act for which the person is responsible." Morality is never accidental.

Free will is a fundamental teaching of the Church. Origen, writing in the third century, puts it very directly: "This is also clearly defined in the teaching of the Church, that every rational soul is possessed of free will and volition." He then goes on to describe this free will as "the power of choosing good and evil." Saint Thomas, writing in the thirteenth century, insists that "every

Christian is bound to hold that acts which issue from a man's own will, namely all his human acts properly so called, are not subject to determinism." Bernard Häring, C.SS.R., writing in the twentieth century, reminds us that "the Church has defined as a dogma of faith that the children of Adam even after the fall are in possession of moral freedom of choice."

This moral freedom of choice means that a person is able to choose or not choose a certain action, or is able to choose freely between two alternative courses of action. If a person is not *free* to choose between good and evil, right and wrong, then there can be no such thing as love or sin or responsibility or crime or punishment. If a person does not have free will, he deserves neither credit nor blame for what he does.

It is in this context that Vatican Council II underlines the enormous importance of freedom: "It is only in freedom that man can turn himself toward that which is good . . . That which is truly freedom is an exceptional sign of the image of God in man. For God willed that man 'should be left in the hand of his own counsel' so that he might of his own accord seek his creator and freely attain his full and blessed perfection by cleaving to him. *Man's dignity therefore requires him to act out of conscious and free choice, as moved and drawn in a personal way from within, and not by blind impulses in himself or by mere external constraint"* (*The Church in the World,* 17).

The poet Dante said that of all the gifts of God to man "most precious, was the liberty of the will." It is because of that gift that we can choose the good and respond to God's love. As is the case with most precious gifts, freedom carries with it great challenges: the challenge to live responsibly, the challenge to struggle against evil, the challenge to grow and mature as Christians.

While we praise and prize this gift of radical freedom, we must at the same time recognize it is not immune from all obstacles and pressures. The free will we have described does not operate in a vacuum. It functions in the real world, where bodily existence and complex emotions and outside influences come into play. Saint Thomas described how ignorance, passion, force, and fear could diminish a person's freedom or even take it away completely. One could think of many examples. Timothy O'Connell gives some up-to-date examples of how force and fear influence freedom when he writes: "The presence of violent force, or the threat of such force, stands in obvious opposition to the exercise of the human act. Whether the case be that of a 'shotgun wedding,' the dire threats of a rapist, or the more subtle pressures of the corporate supervisor against a needy employee, the underlying reality is the same. The presence of force (and the fear it engenders) inhibits and at least partially prevents the clear thinking and free choosing that comprise a really human act'' *(Principles for a Catholic Morality).*

In addition to the fairly obvious obstacles already mentioned, theologians also discuss how other aspects of personality and education exercise subtle influence on freedom: for example, temperament, the functioning of the endocrine glands, drugs, environment, mental disturbance, unconscious motivation, and the like. It is clear that we cannot delve into all of these factors in this short book, but the very naming of them reminds us of the complexity of the human personality and human relationships.

The practical implications of all of this are many. First of all, freedom is a marvelous gift of God, one that makes us human in the fullest sense of the word. Secondly, freedom should be developed and nourished; it should not be endangered by unnecessary mood-altering drugs or unexamined habits. Thirdly, however, the very fact that freedom can be limited should teach us to be mild and cautious in our judgment of others and patient in dealing with ourselves. In the final analysis, as the Gospel teaches, only God can judge an individual. There are many nuances that we do not understand now and may never understand. Finally, we should all seek ways of enhancing human freedom and of avoiding all that diminishes it. For freedom is God's noblest gift to us and, therefore, our most sacred obligation.

The Role of Conscience

In the first chapter we concentrated on "the great law of love." It is vitally important that we keep our vocation to love always before our eyes. Otherwise, like a dried-out cedar tree, our Christian lives become lifeless and heavy. There is great value in having a shining ideal against which to measure the often humdrum decisions of our daily lives.

Yet the law of love is admittedly a quite general norm. In real life we must make many concrete decisions and particular choices each day. How do we bridge the gap between the great law of love on the one hand and our daily judgments and actions on the other? One way is through *conscience*.

Conscience is a very large topic, one about which entire books have been written. For our purposes we want to focus on how the Catholic tradition describes conscience in a twofold way: (1) as absolutely fundamental in understanding the dignity of the human person in his or her relationship with God, and (2) as a practical moral guide in making judgments and decisions in daily life.

The human person, as we have seen, shares in the image of God and is called by God to live in a free and responsible way. God does not force the human person to live responsibly and lovingly, but he does invite and call in the depths of each person's heart. Here, "in the depths of the heart," is where conscience exists.

In a moving statement, Vatican Council II describes this fundamental meaning of conscience: "Deep within his conscience the human person discovers a law which he has not laid upon himself but which he must obey. Its voice, ever calling him to love and to do what is good and to avoid evil, tells him inwardly at the right moment: do this, shun that. For the human person has in his heart a law inscribed by God. His dignity lies in observing this law, and by it he will be judged. Conscience is the most secret core and sanctuary of a person. There he is alone with God whose voice echoes in his depths. In a wonderful manner conscience reveals that law which is fulfilled in the love of God and one's neighbor" (*Church in the World,* 16).

Conscience is, therefore, not something "tacked on" to the human person. It is part of the standard equipment of our human nature. It is an innate or inborn faculty by which we are able to know God's law which, as Saint Paul says, is written in our hearts (Romans 2:15). The term *heart* here refers not simply to the muscular organ of the body, but rather is understood in the biblical sense as "the seat not only of the emotions but also of thoughts and voluntary acts. Thus, the heart represents the whole man" (*The New American Bible,* Glossary). In academic terms, conscience is called "a judgment of the practical reason." But it is not just any kind of judgment; it is a judgment precisely about good and evil, right and wrong.

In popular literature the conscience has been described as "a still small voice within." Vatican Council II seizes on that metaphor to show the intimate relationship between God and the human person. The voice of God echoes in the depths, the most secret core, of the person. The voice of God is not a hollow sound but "a call" to love God and one's neighbor. Yet the voice does not instill such servile fear as to remove freedom. The dignity of the human person consists in this: that he or she can intelligently and *freely* choose God's will and God's law.

The emphasis on freedom is important. "It is through his conscience that man sees and recognizes the demands of the divine law. He is bound to follow this conscience faithfully in all his activity so that he may come to God, who is his last end. Therefore, *he must not be forced to act contrary to his conscience.* Nor must he be prevented from acting according to his conscience, especially in religious matters" (*Religious Liberty,* 3). The conscience is like a sacred sanctuary which should not be violated by alien boots.

With the dignity of conscience thus established, it is necessary to look at another dimension of conscience — namely, how it functions as a practical moral guide. Experience testifies that we make a number of moral judgments and decisions every day. To be sure, some of them are quite routine, but others are crucially important for ourselves and others. Some are controversial, others almost universally agreed upon. In all of these moral judgments, conscience comes into play. On this practical level of human life, conscience may be described as "a personal judgment which decides, from general moral values and principles, that an act I am about to do is morally good or evil because it does or does not conform to God's law of love."

Let us take a simple example. The person ahead of you at the teller's window drops a hundred dollar bill. He is totally unaware of this fact. You could easily pick it up and slip it into your pocket. But you know it doesn't belong to you. Conscience urges the question, "Is it right or wrong for me to take this money?" Eventually you must say yes or no. *How* you arrive at your decision is a critical matter in our understanding of conscience.

An important point to notice is that conscience does not make up the rules of right and wrong. Conscience judges on the basis of some previous moral knowledge or moral value which a person has made his or her own. This previous moral knowledge may come from a number of sources: for example, one's training at home ("Don't take what doesn't belong to you!") or from one's less than admirable peers ("Take it if you can get away with it!") or from the Bible ("You shall not steal!"). The point is that conscience itself is not the judge of what is right and wrong. Conscience is the act by which a person applies a general moral principle to his or her own action here and now.

To return to our example, let us assume that you believe God's commandment about stealing. What would happen, then, is a quick and almost reflex analysis of the situation, along these lines: "God's law says, 'You shall not steal.' Taking this hundred dollar bill would amount to stealing. Therefore (and this is the act of conscience) I will not take it."

Obviously, this example is extremely simple. There are many other situations in which the moral values and principles are not that clear. Ambiguity enters into many of our decisions of conscience. A great deal of discernment is often required to separate out the black from the white and to see the gray in between. That is why the Church places so much emphasis on the formation of conscience.

It is in this context that the term "freedom of conscience" seems to get very confused. If I am an employer, does "freedom of conscience" allow me to disregard the rights of my employees? If a woman is pregnant, does "freedom of conscience" allow her to have an abortion? If I am a father of children, does "freedom of conscience" justify my taking off for Europe while the children lack basic necessities? The answer to these questions has to be no. Conscience is not a law unto itself; it is not a manufacturer of moral values. The values of justice, charity, and truth surely have some objective meaning. While it is certainly true that a person's conscience may err in good faith, as we shall see in the next section, it is also true that an authentic moral life demands that conscience, in the phrase of Cardinal Newman, "reach forward beyond itself" for a knowledge and appreciation of what is right and wrong.

Should Conscience Be Your Guide?

When Jiminy Cricket sang to Pinnochio, "Always let your conscience be your guide," was he giving him good advice? *Should* conscience be our guide? The tradition of the Church would reply that *it all depends*.

Depends on what? It depends on whether one's conscience is *true* or *false*. A *true* conscience is one that is rightly formed, one that is in accord with God's will and God's law. In other words, conscience needs to be guided, directed, enlightened. As the American bishops put it, "We must make decisions of conscience based on prayer, study, consultation, and an understanding of the teaching of the Church" (*To Live in Christ Jesus,* 10).

A *false* conscience, on the other hand, is one that is not in accord with God's law and God's will, but is based on a false understanding of these or on purely selfish interests. A false conscience can come about *through the individual's own fault* (because he or she does not make the necessary effort to discover the truth or overcome evil), or *through ignorance* (because the person does not suspect there is anything wrong with the action or because the necessary information is unknown).

A vincibly false conscience (that is, false through one's own fault) is *not good enough to be our guide*. To follow such a conscience means that we are willing to offend God and his love without even bothering to search for the truth. The woman who casually says, "I'll get an abortion if I feel like it; it's my body," is acting with a vincibly false conscience. The same is true of the businessman who decrees that "you can't worry about morality when you're running a business." With this cliché he has erased the law of God from a good portion of his life.

An invincibly false conscience (*not* through one's own fault), on the other hand, *can* serve as our guide. For we are truly acting in good faith. We have taken our relationship with God seriously, we have done our best. Objectively speaking, it may turn out that what we did was wrong. But we were faithful to the Lord as far as we were able.

Vatican Council II has summarized this teaching about conscience in this way: "In fidelity to conscience, Christians are joined with the rest of humanity in search for the truth and for genuine solutions to the numerous problems that arise in the life of individuals and from social relationships. Hence the more a correct conscience holds sway, the more persons and groups turn away from blind choice and strive to be guided by objective norms of morality. Conscience frequently errs from invincible ignorance without losing its dignity. The same cannot be said of the person who cares little for truth and goodness, or of a conscience which by degrees grows practically sightless as a result of habitual sin'' (*The Church in the Modern World,* 16).

As followers of Christ, the challenge we face is to continue throughout our lives to form our consciences as courageously as possible, to be willing to give up false standards, to set aside prejudices, to let ourselves be measured by God's great law of love. To be sure, the formation of conscience is not always simple. But it is always worthwhile, for it signifies the search for God and his truth.

There are many ways of forming one's conscience. The following helpful hints are indicated by the American bishops in their treatment of conscience:

> Common sense requires that conscientious people be open and humble, ready to learn from the experience and insight of others, willing to acknowledge prejudices and even change their judgments in light of better instruction.
>
> Followers of Jesus will have a realistic approach to conscience. They will accept what Jesus taught and judge things as he judges them.
>
> Where are we to look for the teachings of Jesus, hear his voice and discern his will?
>
> In Scripture, whose books were written under the inspiration of the Holy Spirit. In prayer, where we grow in knowledge and love of Christ and commitment to his service. In the events of human life and history, where Christ and his spirit are at work. In the Church, where all these things converge (*To Live in Christ Jesus,* 10).

Progress in the development of conscience depends very much on attitude. You are disposed to act either positively or negatively toward a person, group, object, situation, or value in accord with your attitudes. Here are four ways to mature in this area:

Learn to love the truth and respect the law of love; both are friends you cannot do without.

Develop the habit of thinking before acting; it takes serious thought to form a judgment.

Determine to base your decisions on rightly ordered charity; ask yourself how these decisions affect your love of God, self, others.

Expand your understanding and use of the gift of prudence; apply common sense to the situation at hand.

Formation of conscience demands much from us. Fidelity to conscience demands even more. But fidelity also gives us much in return. For it has been wisely said that "he who loses his conscience has nothing left worth keeping." Conversely, in the words of Shakespeare, "I feel within me a peace above all earthly dignities — a still and quiet conscience."

I have no way of knowing if Jiminy Cricket would have agreed with my explanation. What it amounts to is that there is more to his song, "Let your conscience be your guide," than first meets the ear.

PART TWO:
LOVE THE LORD
YOUR GOD

I, the Lord, am your God . . . You shall not have other gods besides me . . .

You shall not take the name of the Lord, your God, in vain . . .

Remember to keep holy the sabbath day . . . .

— Book of Exodus

There is no love without hope, no hope without love, and neither hope nor love without faith.

— Saint Augustine

Religion is the virtue by which men show to God due worship and reverence.

— Saint Thomas

God in his goodness grants to everyone the grace of prayer by which he or she is able to obtain all other graces for holiness and salvation.

— Saint Alphonsus

The Lord's Day is the original feast day, and it should be proposed to the faithful and taught to them so that it may become in fact a day of joy and freedom from work.

— Vatican II

Progress in Christian unity will be based on our efforts, our theological work, our repeated steps, and especially on our mutual charity; but it is at the same time a grace of the Lord.

— John Paul II

CHAPTER FOUR
THE WAYS OF WORSHIP

Faith: Responding to God

Like the star which led the Magi to the Child in the stable, faith leads us to God. Faith is the power to know God who has revealed himself to us. Faith is our free response to God's loving revelation of himself. Faith is the surest approach to God; it is in truth the only approach we have.

Faith is possible because God has graciously revealed or manifested himself to us. God reveals himself in many ways, but the fullness of his revelation is in Jesus. "In times past, God spoke in fragmentary and varied ways to our fathers through the prophets; in this, the final age, he has spoken to us through his Son, whom he has made heir of all things and through whom he first created the universe. This Son is the reflection of the Father's glory, the exact representation of the Father's being, and he sustains all things by his powerful word . . ." (Hebrews 1:1-3).

Jesus is the Word of God, the perfect image of the Father. In the Gospel we have the mystery of Jesus in whom God has made known his presence in the world. "I am not ashamed of the gospel. It is the power of God leading everyone who believes in it to salvation . . . For in the gospel is revealed the justice of God which begins and ends with faith; as Scripture says, 'The just man shall live by faith' " (Romans 1:16-17). Through Jesus, God offers the gift of faith to us, the vibrant grace by which we are able to respond "yes" to God's redeeming love.

Everything about Jesus reveals God to us. In the words of Vatican Council II, Jesus "completed and perfected revelation and confirmed it with divine guarantees. He did this by the total fact of his presence and self-manifestation — by words and deeds, by signs and miracles, but above all by his death and glorious resurrection from the dead, and finally by sending the spirit of Truth" (*Divine Revelation*, 4).

Faith is the free human act by which a person commits his or her entire self to God, making the full submission of his or her intellect and will to God who reveals, and willingly assenting to the revelation given by him. It is the Holy Spirit who enlightens our minds so that we can see through the eyes of faith. It is the same Spirit, the Spirit of Truth, who guides us to all truth (see John 16:13). Faith is not static but dynamic: it seeks to know God more and more deeply; it strives to experience God as completely as possible in this life.

God's revelation was entrusted first to the apostolic community. The importance of faith is underlined both in the Acts of the Apostles and in the writings of Paul. To be a Christian is to be a believer. To be a believer is to accept the teaching of the apostles: faith in the Lord Jesus and in the power of his grace. (See Acts of the Apostles 11:17 and 15:11.) The task of the apostles was to keep the Gospel alive within the community. The apostles, in their turn, left bishops as their successors, "handing over to them their teaching role."

As in the beginning, so now: God's revelation is found in the community of believers which is the Church. The chief function of the Church is to hand on to each new generation the revelation of God. This revelation, according to Vatican Council II, is contained both in Scripture ("the speech of God as it is put down in writing under the breath of the Holy Spirit") and Tradition ("the word of God which has been entrusted to the apostles by Christ the Lord and the Holy Spirit").

"Sacred Tradition and sacred Scripture make up a single sacred deposit of the word of God, which is entrusted to the Church. By adhering to it the entire holy people, united to its pastors, remains always faithful to the teaching of the apostles, to the brotherhood, to the breaking of the bread and the prayers, as in Acts 2:42" (*Divine Revelation*, 10).

But in the Church, as Paul clearly teaches, there are many gifts and many offices. According to Catholic teaching, one of the offices in the Church is "the teaching office" (in Latin, *magisterium*). "But the task of giving authentic interpretation of the Word of God, whether in its written form or in the form of Tradition, has been entrusted to the living teaching authority of the Church alone. Its authority in this matter is exercised in the name of Jesus Christ. Yet this *magisterium* is not superior to the Word of God, but its servant. It teaches only what has been handed on to it . . . It is clear, therefore, that in the supremely wise arrangement of God, sacred Tradition, sacred Scripture and the Magisterium of the Church are so connected and associated that one of them cannot stand without the others" (*Divine Revelation,* 10).

Saint Teresa of Avila considered herself richly blessed because she was "a daughter of the Church." In our times, it is not uncommon to see sons and daughters of the Church turn away from her in bitterness and anger. To be sure, the community of the Church, because it is made up of weak men and women like ourselves and because it is a part of the broken world, is always in need of reformation and renewal. But the Church is still our spiritual home. It is the place where we find God and his revelation of himself. Bernard Häring, C.SS.R., writes on this question: "That the Church has weaknesses and imperfections is no reason for refusal to love her and listen to her . . . We ourselves have made false assessments many times and have failed in many ways, but this does not permit the Church to stop loving us or to care for us less . . . To leave the Church in protest means that we leave behind Saint Francis of Assisi and the whole choir of saints who were faithful to the Church on earth and pray for her now in heaven. It means separating ourselves from Mother Teresa of Calcutta and so many extraordinary people of today's Church. It means even leaving Mary, the mother of Jesus and of the Church" (*In Pursuit of Holiness*).

While it is possible to sin directly against faith, the far more common error is a benign neglect of faith. Faith becomes like a museum piece hanging on the wall, a relic from the past. We speak often of the *life* of faith. Like all life, faith needs nourishment if it is to grow. Faith must be nourished through study, reading, dialogue, prayer. If one never studies the Scriptures or the teaching of the Church, if one does not seek to penetrate the mystery of God, then one can expect that faith will gradually die. It is hard to see that an immature faith (one suitable for childhood) could be of much help to an adult in the world of today.

Doubts of faith, however, need not cause its death. Many believers experience doubts in one form or another. We are dealing, after all, with the unspeakable mystery of God and trying to comprehend him and his works in fragile human language. The dogmas (or teachings) of the Church are formulations of divine truth. They express the truth about God as exactly as it can be expressed in human terms. But they are complex at times and can be misunderstood. Because of our background or the type of education we have had, they can seem not to make sense. Doubts or difficulties must be dealt with. Saint Alphonsus suggested it was better to confront them than to ignore them. It is especially helpful to confront them with the help of a theological or spiritual guide who is steeped in the tradition of the Catholic faith. At all times we should remember, however, that doubts do not of themselves take away the grandeur of the free human response to God.

Finally, it is important to *express* our faith often, especially in the context of community. Each Sunday's liturgy calls us, as the People of God, to make our profession of faith. In private, too, it is an excellent practice to pray the Act of Faith on a regular basis. There are a number of different forms of the Act of Faith. Here is a brief but beautiful one: "O my God, I firmly believe that you are one God in three Persons, Father, Son, and Holy Spirit; I believe that your divine Son became man and died for our sins, and that he will come to judge the living and the dead. I believe these and all the truths which the Catholic Church teaches, because you revealed them, who can neither deceive nor be deceived."

Hope: Trusting in God

I once had a theology professor who used to say that the forgotten person of the Blessed Trinity was the Holy Spirit, the forgotten sacrament was Confirmation, and the forgotten theological virtue was the virtue of hope! In recent times, it seems that the Holy Spirit and the sacrament of Confirmation have made a comeback, but the virtue of hope is still too easily forgotten.

The anchor is the symbol of hope. "Like a sure and firm anchor," says the author of Hebrews, "that hope extends . . ." (Hebrews 6:19). The anchor was, of course, the symbol of stability. The stability of our hope comes *not* from ourselves, *not* from our strength of virtue or from our optimistic feelings but from God. God is the ground of our being, the rock on which our hope stands.

This is a significant point in our spiritual struggle. The virtue of hope does not depend on our good feelings. Like heat lightning in the summer sky, our feelings come and go, flash and fail. We certainly have no absolute control over them. We know from experience that some days we feel optimistic, other days we don't. Some people, for example, have a predominantly melancholic or pensive temperament. They tend to feel blue more often than they feel orange! But this does not signify that they have no virtue of hope.

The point here is not to put our feelings down. Feelings are important in the moral life. Feelings tell us a lot about ourselves and our relationships. It is helpful to be "tuned in" to our feelings. They are not, however, the foundation of our hope.

Our hope rests on a much more solid foundation: the Resurrection of our Lord Jesus Christ from the dead! The Resurrection was not only a sign of the glorification of Jesus by the Father; it is also the guarantee of *our* final resurrection. It is the source of all our hope. "If we have died with Christ, we believe that we are also to live with him" (Romans 6:8).

Our incorporation into the death and Resurrection of Christ is brought about through the Easter sacrament, the sacrament of Baptism, the sacrament of hope! "Through baptism into his death we were buried with him, so that, just as Christ was raised from the dead by the glory of the Father, we too might live a new life" (Romans 6:4). As baptized members of the Body of Christ, we have a *certain hope* that we, too, shall rise glorious with Christ on the Last Day.

The virtue of hope may be seen to refer to our past, our present, and our future. Fulton Oursler has said that "we crucify ourselves between two thieves: the fear of yesterday and the dread of tomorrow." There is also the struggle of today. Hope touches all of these realities. It is the virtue by which we confidently expect the forgiveness of our past sins, because of the gracious mercy of our God, because we have been redeemed by the blood of Christ. "Realize that you were delivered from the futile way of life your fathers handed on to you, not by any diminishable sum of silver or gold, but by Christ's blood beyond all price . . . It is through him that you are believers in God, the God who raised him from the dead and gave him glory. Your faith and hope, then, are centered in God'' (1 Peter 1:18-21).

Hope is also the virtue by which we confidently expect eternal life, the fullness of glory, and all the means to attain it, because God is faithful to his promises and can neither deceive nor be deceived. "If our hopes in Christ are limited to this life only, we are the most pitiable of men. But as it is, Christ is now raised from the dead, the first fruits of those who have fallen asleep. Death came through a man; hence the resurrection of the dead comes through a man also. Just as in Adam all die, so in Christ all will come to life again" (1 Corinthians 15:19-22).

As we saw in chapter 2, it is possible for us men and women to choose eternal death rather than eternal life. That is the ultimate tragedy of sin: that we are able to turn away from God in a fundamental way. Yet God's grace is sufficient for us, if only we will accept it. "He said to me, 'My grace is enough for you, for in weakness power reaches perfection.' And so I willingly boast of my weaknesses instead, that the power of Christ may rest upon me" (2 Corinthians 12:9).

The virtue of hope does not ensure, of course, that we will never experience trials and tribulations and temptations. All of us must walk at times in the dark valleys of life. All of us experience in a personal way the dark cloud of evil that hangs over the world since the fall of Adam. Hope is not a quick fix against all suffering. Rather, the virtue of hope affirms that, no matter how we feel or what sufferings we face, God is always with us and his grace is sufficient for us. The psalmist, who so often puts into words the profound experiences of the human heart, beautifully expresses the meaning of hope:

> The LORD is my shepherd; I shall not want.
> In verdant pastures he gives me repose;
> Beside restful waters he leads me;
>   he refreshes my soul . . .
> Even though I walk in the dark valley
>   I fear no evil; for you are at my side
> With your rod and your staff
>   that give me courage.   (Psalm 23:1-4)

Not only does the virtue of hope color our personal sufferings, however; it also affects our vision of the world. The Christian vision embraces "a new heaven and a new earth," God's dwelling place among his people. "He shall wipe every tear from their eyes, and there shall be no more death or mourning, crying out or pain, for the former world has passed away" (Revelation 21:4). Yet our hope for this kingdom which is to come does not relieve us of the responsibility to build up the community of mankind here and now. "Far from diminishing our concern to develop this earth, the expectancy of a new earth should spur us on, for it is here that the body of a new human family grows, foreshadowing in some way the age which is to come" (*Church in the Modern World,* 39). The virtue of hope urges us to make our contribution to a better world now.

What was said of the virtue of faith applies to the virtue of hope as well. It must be nourished. Hope holds a delicate balance between despair on the one hand and presumption on the other. Despair means giving up on God and his love and his promises. The world of despair is a dark, dank world without sunshine. Presumption, which at first sight seems to be a brave new world, means basing our hope on a false foundation, such as our own ability alone. Sooner or later, the house of presumption falls.

The Christian tradition encourages us to nourish the virtue of hope by prayer: prayer in general and the prayer of hope in particular. This prayer may be brief and quick: "My God, I place my hope in you!" Or it may be more formal, as in this example: "My God, relying on your infinite goodness and promises, I hope to obtain pardon for my sins, the help of your grace and life everlasting, through the merits of Jesus Christ, my Lord and Redeemer."

Religion: Relating to God

The word religion is probably from a Latin word meaning "to bind oneself to." Religion is a way of relating to God. In the classical definition, it is the virtue which treats of our worship of God who is our Lord and Creator. Because God made all things and has supreme dominion over all, he is deserving of our special worship. "In the beginning was the Word; the Word was in God's presence, and the Word was God. He was present to God in the beginning. Through him all things came into being, and apart from him nothing came to be" (John 1:1-3).

Not only were we created by God, but we are kept in existence by him. "For the God who made the world and all that is in it, the Lord of heaven and earth, does not dwell in sanctuaries made by human hands; nor does he receive man's service as if he were in need of it. Rather, it is he who gives to all life and breath and everything else" (Acts 17:24-25). Before the beginning of anything else, the only true God was existing. He transcends all that is, and all that is has its being from him.

Because we recognize God as our Creator and because we acknowledge our dependence on him, we are ready and willing to worship him and him alone. "I, the LORD, am your God, who brought you out of the land of Egypt, that place of slavery. You shall not have other gods besides me . . . you shall not bow down before them or worship them . . ." (Exodus 20:2-5). Religion is that virtue which urges us to worship God as he deserves and wants to be worshiped. It is our way of relating to God.

Like everything that is authentically human, true religion must be both *internal* and *external*. The internal is the very heart of religion; without it, we have only a corpse. That is to say, before religious *practices* (for example, sacrifice, prayers, sacraments) comes the deep inner conviction of faith: that God is Creator and Lord, that he has revealed himself in the works of creation and especially in Jesus Christ, the Son of God. True religion, like true morality, is above all a matter of the heart! This does not mean that religion is a sweet sentiment or a warm feeling. But it does mean that there must be an inner conviction and "a ready will."

Saint Thomas defines "true devotion" as the will to give oneself wholeheartedly to things concerning the worship and service of God. We often say that it is not so much the *gift* that is given at Christmas or birthday time but, rather, the thought or, more precisely, the love behind the gift. So, too, in religion: the will to worship God, the love that prompts the act, is what matters most!

Yet true religion is also *external*. Saint Thomas says that God "ought to be worshiped not only by internal but also by external acts . . . In divine worship it is necessary to make use of bodily things, that the human being may be aroused, as by signs, to the spiritual acts by which he is united to God." Just as an artist is not content with an image in his mind but labors to express it on canvas, so we strive to express our relationship with God in external acts of worship.

The internal and external dimensions of religion come together, ideally, in the public worship of the Church known as *the sacred liturgy*. The liturgy is the Church at prayer, offering adoration, praise, and thanksgiving to God. "For it is the liturgy through which, especially in the divine sacrifice of the Eucharist, 'the work of redemption is accomplished,' and it is through the liturgy, especially, that the faithful are enabled to express in their lives and manifest to others the mystery of Christ and the real nature of the true Church" (*The Sacred Liturgy,* 2).

The liturgy is called the summit toward which the activity of the Church is directed and the fount from which all her power flows, mainly because in the liturgy we are joined to Christ himself. "The liturgy, then, is rightly seen as an exercise of the priestly office of Jesus Christ. It involves the presentation of man's sanctification under the guise of signs perceptible to the senses and its accomplishment in ways appropriate to each of these signs. In it full public worship is performed by the Mystical Body of Jesus Christ, that is, by the Head and his members" (*The Sacred Liturgy,* 7).

What is included in the term *liturgy?* First, the celebration of the sacrifice and sacrament of the Eucharist. (We will return to a consideration of this great mystery in a later chapter.) Secondly, the celebration of the other sacraments (the external signs instituted by Christ to bring his grace to us). And finally, the "liturgy of the hours" or the divine office (a set form of hymns, psalms, readings, and prayers recited at particular times of the day). According to the teaching of the Church, the primacy of the liturgy is due to the living presence of Christ in it. Vatican Council II explains this beautifully: "Christ is always present in his Church, especially in her liturgical celebrations. He is present in the sacrifice of the Mass not only in the person of the minister, 'the same now offering through the ministry of priests, who formerly offered himself on the cross,' but especially in the eucharistic species. By his power he is present in the sacraments so that when anyone baptizes it is really Christ himself who baptizes. He is present in his Word since it is he himself who speaks when the holy scriptures are read in the Church. Lastly, he is present when the Church prays and sings, for he has promised 'where two or three are gathered together in my name there I am in the midst of them!' " (*The Sacred Liturgy,* 7)

Recently I had an experience of worship which thrilled me and made me long for more. I celebrated the Eucharist with a group of faith-filled men, women, and children. All of us brought to the celebration, as best we could, a spirit of "true devotion." All of us expressed this inner spirit by bringing our gifts, our voices, our gestures, to the celebration. I believe the great Saint Thomas would have said: "Yes, my friends, that is the meaning of religion!"

Prayer: Communicating with God

One of the foremost acts of religion is prayer. Prayer was central to the life and teaching of Jesus. (See, for example, Luke 4:1-13, 22:29-46; John 16:23.) From the very beginning of the Christian community, Christians have thought about prayer, talked about it, and practiced it. In that sense, though the fundamentals of prayer are quite simple, the description and experience of it are rich and varied.

Perhaps the most basic description of prayer is that given by Saint Augustine: "Prayer is communication with God." As an aspect of religion, prayer is a way of relating to God, a way of being in touch with him. Prayer is based on the faith conviction that, though we cannot see God with our bodily eyes, God is present to us, interested in us, loving us. Conscious of his loving presence, we communicate with him in a personal and loving way.

Like a brilliant diamond, however, prayer has many facets. Like the shadow of a willow tree, prayer takes many forms. It is helpful to review some of the ways of praying, as taught to us by the Church and by the living example of many Christians. It is customary to distinguish, first of all, *common* prayer and *private* prayer. Common prayer may be further distinguished into *liturgical* prayer (the public and official prayer of the Church) and *nonliturgical* prayer (common prayer in accord with the teaching of the Church but not a part of the official prayer of the Church).

Private prayer, too, may be divided in many ways. For our purposes here we may distinguish between *meditative* prayer (also called contemplative) and *relational* prayer (the "praying always" of the Scriptures). It goes without saying that *all* prayer, whatever its form, must come from the heart. Otherwise, it is not prayer.

In the last chapter we saw that liturgical prayer is the "summit toward which the activity of the Church is directed . . . the fount from which all her powers flow.'' Liturgical prayer is the highest form of prayer. There are, however, other forms of prayer in common. These vary widely and have a definite place in the Church, provided that they are ''so drawn up that they harmonize with the liturgical seasons, accord with the sacred liturgy, are in some ways derived from it, and lead people to it . . .'' (*The Sacred Liturgy*, 13).

Such ''popular devotions,'' as they are often called, would include Solemn Eucharistic Adoration (formerly called Forty Hours Devotion), public Stations of the Cross, devotion in honor of Mary (such as the Perpetual Help Novena), and many more. Common prayer is especially fitting in the family, ''the little Church.'' Christian tradition recommends: reading and reflection on the Scriptures, grace before and after meals, the recitation of the family rosary and other common prayers. All such forms of prayer are designed to bring people together as a community of God's people, a community that shares its faith and expresses its love.

Yet, while the communal dimension of prayer is always important, we must not neglect the *personal* dimension. ''The Christian is indeed called to pray with others, but he must also enter his room to pray to his Father in secret'' (*The Sacred Liturgy*, 12). This kind of prayer goes by many names: meditation, contemplation, centering prayer. Saint Alphonsus Liguori, called the Doctor of Prayer, considered this form of prayer practically necessary for the living of a fervent Christian life. ''Without mental prayer,'' he writes, ''there is no light; we walk in the darkness.'' Many other saints have written in the same vein.

What we have described so far indicates a certain *formality* about prayer: a certain time and place, with others or by oneself. Saint Paul instructs us, however, to ''Rejoice always, never cease praying'' (1 Thessalonians 5:16-17). It seems evident that Paul is not referring to formal prayer. Given our busy lives, such prayer would be impossible. Rather, Paul is exhorting us to become more and more *aware* of God's presence in our lives, more conscious of our relationship with him. The saints spoke often of a ''spirit of recollection'' wherein God's presence and love become, as it were, the atmosphere or environment in which we live. From time to time, no matter how busy we are, we turn naturally to God, as a flower turns to the sunlight. In this way the bond of love grows stronger.

Not only are the forms of prayer many, so also are its *purposes*. If we contemplate the prayer forms of the liturgy, we see that certain broad categories of prayer emerge. These are: adoration, thanksgiving, contrition, petition.

Adoration expresses in the form of prayer what we *believe* about God in our minds and hearts. The prayer of adoration is a way of saying, "How wonderful is our God!" The Psalms are full of such joyful prayers: "Bless the LORD, O my soul! O LORD, my God, you are great indeed!" (Psalm 104:1). The "Glory to God in the highest," which we as the People of God pray on most Sundays of the year, is a marvelous prayer of adoration and praise. "Lord God, heavenly King, almighty God and Father, we worship you, we give you thanks, we praise you for your glory." The prayer of adoration and praise is a "specialty" of the charismatic prayer groups which have become so widespread in recent years and so meaningful to many people. Their spotlighting of such prayer is a good reminder for all of us.

Thanksgiving is a simple way of recognizing God as the Giver of all good gifts. One of the common perversities of human nature is to take things for granted. Some people never say thanks to anyone, God included! It is important for us, as Christians, to have a grateful memory, to count our blessings — for example, our health, our gifts and talents, our faith, our family and friends — and as we become aware of them to give thanks to God. "Give thanks to the LORD, for he is good, for his mercy endures forever (Psalm 136:1).

The prayer of *Contrition* assumes that we are all sinners, that we all fail in love. It is a cry for the Lord's forgiveness. Jesus instructs us to pray in this way: "Our Father in heaven . . . forgive us the wrong we have done as we forgive those who wrong us" (Matthew 6:9,12).

The prayer of *Petition* is frequently recommended by Jesus. "Ask, and you will receive. Seek, and you will find. Knock, and it will be opened to you" (Matthew 7:7). This prayer acknowledges our dependence on God, our need for his grace and blessings. Obviously, the point of the prayer of petition is *not to inform* God of our needs but, rather, to acknowledge him as the source of all good and to lay ourselves open to his love.

It is clear, then, that prayer takes many forms and has many purposes. It is almost impossible to imagine a Christian life without prayer. One of the most hopeful "signs of the times" is, in my opinion, the new interest in prayer that one finds in all age groups and all segments of society. Prayer is essential to the Christian life. Without it we gradually lose sight of our intimate relationship with God and our dignity as followers of Christ. Prayer renews our vision of faith, enlivens our desire to love, gives us strength for the journey of life.

Prayer: Common Questions

Like grass that pops up in the cracks of the sidewalk, certain questions about prayer seem to arise whenever the subject is discussed. Some questions arise often because we are dealing with great mysteries, for example, the mystery of the way God works in our lives. Others arise because of basic misunderstandings of a historical nature; for example, why do Catholics pray to the Virgin Mary? In this section we will pose some of the commonly asked questions and give a brief response to them.

Q. *Why are my prayers not always answered?*

We can suggest this answer: Our prayers are always answered, but not always in the way we desire or expect. Saint Augustine, one of the Church's great theologians, makes a distinction. He says that God will infallibly answer our prayers that are truly for our "eternal beatitude," our essential happiness. At other times, because we ask for what will not bring about this happiness, God mercifully refuses our request. What we are praying for might indeed be opposed to our essential happiness. "The physician knows better than the patient what is necessary for health." Jesus used a similar analogy: If we can trust an earthly father to give good things to his children, and not evil ones, how much more can we trust our heavenly Father to give us what is good? (See Luke 11:11-13.)

Another aspect of this question may be this: Sometimes our prayers are not answered because we do not pray with perseverance. Jesus told a number of parables "on the necessity of praying always and not losing heart." One parable was about the man who knocked on his neighbor's door until he finally got up and gave him bread — not out of friendship but just to get rid of him!

Another was about the dishonest judge who yields to the widow's request because he is tired of her (see Luke 18:1-8). Saint Augustine says, "Perhaps your prayers are not heard because you have ceased asking."

Q. *Is there a strict obligation to pray at certain times, for example, morning and night, before and after meals, etc?*

There is no general law of the Church commanding morning and night prayers, prayers before and after meals, etc. These times are suggested as being good times for most people to pray. To omit these prayers is not sinful.

On a more general level, we can say, I believe, that *prayer is necessary for salvation.* Certainly many of the great saints, for example, Saint Alphonsus Liguori, taught this doctrine. Many theologians have taught that a person is bound to pray "frequently" in the course of his life, but ordinarily they do not go into detail.

It should be noted, however, that the obligation to attend Mass on Sundays (a serious law of the Church) clearly implies an obligation to pray at that time.

The question of "strict obligation" tends to lead us into many legalistic distinctions. If prayer is a way of communicating with God, and if we are serious about our relationship with him, prayer will be a "natural" and frequent part of our lives.

Q. *Why does the Catholic Church allow prayer to the Blessed Virgin Mary and the saints?*

Although this question never seems to be "answered" for some people, Vatican Council II gives an excellent explanation for the Church's tradition and practice. "The Church has always believed that the apostles and Christ's martyrs, who gave the supreme witness of faith and charity by the shedding of their blood, are closely united with us in Christ; she has always venerated them, together with the Blessed Virgin Mary and the holy angels, with a special love, and has asked piously for the help of their intercession . . . It is most fitting, therefore, that we love those friends and co-heirs of Jesus Christ who are also our brothers and benefactors, and that we give due thanks to God for them, 'humbly invoking them, and having recourse to their prayers, their aid and help in obtaining from God through his Son, Jesus Christ, our Lord, our only Redeemer and Savior, the benefits we need' '' (*The Church,* 50).

The Council is concerned that any abuses, excesses, or defects that may have crept in be eliminated. It reminds us that "the authentic cult of the saints does not consist so much in a multiplicity of external acts, but rather in a more intense practice of our love, whereby . . . we seek from the saints 'example in their way of life, fellowship in their communion, and the help of their intercession.' '' With these cautions in mind, "let the faithful be taught that our communion with those in heaven, provided it is understood in the full light of faith, in no way diminishes the worship of adoration given to God the Father, through Christ, in the Spirit; on the contrary, it greatly enriches it" (*The Church,* 51).

Concerning Mary, the Mother of God, Vatican II points out that "she is rightly honored by a special cult in the Church . . . This cult, for all its uniqueness, differs essentially from the cult of adoration, which is offered equally to the Incarnate Word and to the Father and the Holy Spirit, and is most favorable to it. The various forms of piety toward the Mother of God, which the Church has approved within the limits of sound and orthodox doctrine . . . ensure that while the mother is honored, the Son through whom all things have their being (Colossians 1:15-16) and in whom it has pleased the Father that all fullness should dwell is rightly known, loved and glorified and his commandments are observed" (*The Church,* 66).

Other Gods?

From the days of the first martyrs, who were sometimes put to death for refusing to burn incense before idols, till the present preoccupation with the occult, the Christian community has seen a lot! It has been forced to reflect on practices which are against the virtue of religion and contrary to the first commandment.

Saint Thomas Aquinas turned his astute mind to an analysis of these practices. He distinguished many ways in which the true God is dishonored and other ways in which creatures are given the honor that belongs to God alone. Other theologians, before and after Thomas, have done the same thing. While it would be beyond the scope of this book to attempt a summary of all this material, a brief review of the highlights might be helpful.

Idolatry may be defined as giving to a created object (image, idol) the honor that belongs to God alone. Idolatry in this sense is not very common these days. Many theologians believe, however, that there is need for an updated appreciation of how idolatry appears in the modern world. While the Canaanite god Baal (represented by a bull) may not have many followers, the question can be asked if *other* creatures have taken his place. Theologian Paul Meagher, O.P., makes this point very well: "In modern times idolatry in any strict sense of the word is not a sin of frequent occurrence in the Western world, although it appears to have a place in the practices of devil worship and Satanism. For the most part, however, modern man's closest acquaintance with it is likely to be in metaphorical form, i.e., the idolatry into which one falls when he attributes supreme value to something less than God and pursues it as his ultimate goal in life" (*New Catholic Encyclopedia*).

Is idolatry too strong a word for the way some people "worship" money and material possessions? Jesus spoke of the danger of letting money be our master: "No man can serve two masters. He will either hate one and love the other or be attentive to one and despise the other. You cannot give yourself to God and money" (Matthew 6:24). Gross avarice seems to make gods of created things, while at the same time developing an illusion that one is independent of the true God.

Saint Paul spoke of "that lust which is idolatry" (Colossians 3:5) and declared: "Make no mistake about this: no fornicator, no unclean or lustful person — in effect an idolater — has any inheritance in the kingdom of Christ and of God" (Ephesians 5:5). Is "idolatry" too strong a word for the glorification of self-centered sex and hard-core pornography so rampant in our society?

Satanism (referred to above) signifies the cult which honors Satan with religious ceremonies in mockery of Christian rites. That such "devil worship" actually exists seems beyond dispute. Moreover, some very fine young people have been caught in its web.

Superstition is far more common than idolatry. (Think how often we hear about the number 13, black cats, rabbit's feet, and the like!) Superstition implies expecting from some created thing a power it does not possess. A superstitious person tries to obtain from a source (object, person) some information or benefit which

God alone can give. Superstition takes almost innumerable forms: fortune-telling (by palmists, phrenologists, numerologists, etc.); astrology; spiritism or spiritualism (knowledge from spirits through séances) and many others.

Most theologians seem to feel that these practices are not taken seriously in our society; no dishonor to God is intended. It is hard to know. Certainly there are Christians who take fortune-tellers seriously, who base serious decisions of their lives on their horoscopes, who believe in the messages of séances. There seems to be a profound lack of faith in the lives of such people. The further they stray from true faith and true religion, the closer they seem to draw to superstition. Objectively speaking, it is hard to see how true religion and serious superstition can exist in the same person.

Even the practice of religion itself, however, can be infected by superstition. A Catholic can be superstitious about the use of medals, statues, chain letters, or vigil lights. As John A. Hardon, S.J., remarks: "The Church warns its members about placing unwarranted trust in a precise number of prayers, genuflections, or lighted candles, when the person relies on the number alone, like the revolutions of the praying wheel in Buddhism" (*The Catholic Catechism*). The Catholic tradition (repeated in Vatican Council II) does not prohibit the use of objects (such as the statue of a saint) or popular practices (such as a novena in honor of Mary) as long as these are seen as *helps* to devotion and not ends in themselves.

Much more could be said about idolatry and superstition. Ultimately, however, the question seems one of *trust*. In whom, in what, shall we place our trust? In money or Satan or fortune-tellers or astrology or séances? Jesus said: "Look at the birds in the sky. They do not sow or reap, they gather nothing into barns; yet your heavenly Father feeds them. Are not you more important than they? Which of you by worrying can add a moment to his life-span? . . . Your heavenly Father knows all that you need. Seek first his kingship over you, his way of holiness, and all these things will be given you besides" (Matthew 6:26-27,32-33).

God's Holy Name

What's in a name? The people of Israel thought that names were special. They had a great reverence for names, whether of places or persons or God himself. When God revealed himself to Moses, he described himself as "I Am Who Am." From that time on, the name *Yahweh* (which means "he is") expressed God's absolute and unchanging Being with all its perfection and power. The Israelites had such reverence for this name that they seldom spoke it. Once a year the high priest in the temple pronounced the name *Yahweh*, but in daily prayer and instruction the Israelites used other names, such as *Adonai* (The Lord). The name of Yahweh, they believed, should always be spoken reverently; it must not be profaned (Leviticus 24:11) or spoken in vain (Exodus 20:7).

The name of *Jesus* was held in similar reverence and esteem. ". . . God highly exalted him and bestowed on him the name above every other name, so that at Jesus' name every knee must bend in the heavens, on the earth, and under the earth . . ." (Philippians 2:9-10). The apostles, we are told, baptized, preached, worked miracles in the name of Jesus. When Peter and John were on their way to the temple one day, a lame man pleaded for a donation. Looking on him kindly, Peter said: "I have neither silver nor gold, but what I have I give you! In the name of Jesus Christ the Nazorean, walk!" (Acts 3:6) The man began to walk and praise God, and all the people were amazed at what had happened.

The Christian community prays in the name of Jesus (see John 14:13). The Christian person acts and performs good deeds "in the name of Jesus." "Whatever you do, whether in speech or in action, do it in the name of the Lord Jesus . . ." (Colossians 3:17). The name of Jesus is the principle of unity in the Church. "Where two or three are gathered in my name, there am I in their midst" (Matthew 18:20).

Time has not tarnished the name of God nor taken away the beauty and power of the name of Jesus. To speak God's name prayerfully is to honor him. To say his name reverently is an act of love. To call his name in temptation is a cry for help. To whisper the name of Jesus is to draw close to him.

Unfortunately, however, there are also many ways in which people dishonor the name of God and the name of Jesus. It might be helpful for us to make a brief review of the offences which dishonor God by abusing his name in one way or another:

1. *Blasphemy* is the intentional insulting of God or a denial of his goodness, as when one would seriously say that God is unjust or unmerciful. Blasphemy is the other side of the coin of worship. It is the gravest dishonor to God's name and person.

2. *Perjury* is the calling on God to witness to what one knows to be a lie. Perjury is said to be quite common in our court system, but it certainly dishonors God and erodes the trust and confidence necessary for peaceful living in society.
3. *Cursing,* in the strict sense, is asking God to wish evil on someone or to damn someone for all eternity. It is evident what a perversion of love this would involve. ("Cursing" or "cussing" is sometimes used to describe vulgar or crude language. This entails a problem of good manners rather than morality.)
4. *Profanity* is a disrespectful use of God's name, using the name of God or Jesus to express anger or fear or surprise. It is unfortunate how many believing people allow the name of God or Jesus to become normal expletives in their conversation. In terms of general religious behavior, this bad habit deserves more serious attention than it usually receives.

On the positive side, there are many practices and customs that praise the name of the Lord. For example: bowing our heads whenever the name of Jesus is spoken, saying a prayer of praise whenever we hear God's name abused. These and other practices have a legitimate place in adult life.

Finally, one sees frequent reference these days to "the Jesus Prayer." This is an aspect of contemplative prayer in which slow and rhythmic breathing is considered a help to the one praying. James Borst, M.H.M., gives a brief description of this: "A suitable prayer that is repeated helps to sustain your quiet and rhythmic breathing. You can speak the words (with the lips or, better, mentally) either while breathing in or breathing out or both. In view of the rhythmic breathing, the prayer should have a certain cadence or rhythm, allowing it to be sustained by the rhythm of the breathing. The best-known example of this is the Jesus Prayer; the text consists either in a repetition of the holy name, 'Jesus, Jesus, Jesus,' or in the words, 'Jesus, Son of the living God, have mercy on me, a sinner.' It is sustained rhythmically with your quiet breathing, again and again, while your awareness remains on the Savior" *(Contemplative Prayer)*. The second commandment is thus more than a warning not to take the name of the Lord in vain. It is also an invitation to respond to God's name with love and praise. "It is good to give thanks to the LORD, to sing praise to your name, Most High . . ." (Psalm 92:2).

CHAPTER FIVE
SUNDAY IS SPECIAL

Holy Eucharist: Sacrifice and Sacrament

The Jewish people held the seventh day of the week, the Sabbath, in special reverence. It was their day of worship and spiritual renewal. This reverence grew out of the example of the Lord himself in the story of creation: "Since on the seventh day God was finished with the work he had been doing, he rested on the seventh day from all the work he had undertaken. So God blessed the seventh day and made it holy, because on it he rested from all the work he had done in creation" (Genesis 2:2-3).

The Jewish people paid attention to the Lord when he said: "Take care to keep holy the sabbath day as the LORD, your God, commanded you. Six days you may labor and do all your work; but the seventh day is the sabbath of the LORD, your God. No work may be done then . . ." (Deuteronomy 5:12-14). Though the laws of the Sabbath were very strict, the people followed them willingly. Even to this day many Jews observe the Sabbath with great reverence.

Very early in its experience the Christian community transferred the Sabbath to the first day of the week, Sunday, and called it the Lord's Day. (See Revelation 1:10.) At the risk of oversimplification, we may say that there were two basic reasons for this change. The first was that the Christians considered themselves "the new people of God" and did not feel bound by the old law. The second reason was that the most memorable events of the

Christian life took place on the first day of the week. Writing in the second century, Saint Justin Martyr declared: "Sunday, indeed, is the day on which we hold our common assembly because it is the first day on which God, transforming the darkness and matter, created the world; and our Savior Jesus Christ arose from the dead on the same day."

For the Christian, therefore, the first day of every week is a special day. It is the Lord's Day or, according to an ancient saying in the Church, "a little Easter." Sunday is special in several ways. First of all, it is the day on which the Christian community comes together for the celebration of "the paschal mystery," the holy Mass. In the words of Vatican Council II, "On this day Christ's faithful are bound to come together into one place. They should listen to the word of God and take part in the Eucharist, thus calling to mind the passion, resurrection, and glory of the Lord Jesus, and giving thanks to God who has 'begotten them again through the resurrection of Christ from the dead, unto a living hope' (1 Peter 1:3)" (*Constitution on the Liturgy*, 106).

The celebration of the Eucharist is the central act of Christian worship. Robert Hugh Benson, novelist and poet, expressed this profound truth in a simple way:

For Holy Mass is better far
Than earth or moon or sea or star
Or all things that within them are!

A significant chapter of the *Constitution on the Liturgy*, the first major document produced by Vatican Council II, is called "The Most Sacred Mystery of the Eucharist." There the faith of the Church is beautifully expressed: "At the Last Supper, on the night when he was betrayed, our Savior instituted the Eucharistic Sacrifice of his Body and Blood. He did this in order to perpetuate the sacrifice of the Cross throughout the centuries until he should come again, and so entrust to his beloved spouse, the Church, a memorial of his death and resurrection: a sacrament of love, a bond of charity, a paschal banquet in which Christ is consumed, the mind is filled with grace, and a pledge of future glory is given to us" (47).

It is not a poetic exaggeration to say that the Mass perpetuates the sacrifice of the Cross throughout the centuries. For on the Cross, Christ was the Victim; in the Mass, Christ is still the

Victim. On the Cross, Christ was the High Priest, offering himself to the Father; in the Mass, Christ is still the High Priest, offering himself to the Father, but acting now through human agents. On the Cross, Christ offered himself to glorify God and make reparation for sin; in the Mass, Christ still offers himself for these same reasons.

The Mass, far from being merely an obligation, is an incredible privilege, for in it we are able to join with Christ in his sacrifice to the Father and to offer ourselves along with him. It is, moreover, our privilege to receive our risen Lord, the Body and Blood of Christ, in Holy Communion. "Every time, then, you eat this bread and drink this cup, you proclaim the death of the Lord until he comes!" (1 Corinthians 11:26)

Perhaps one of the most important practical thrusts of Vatican II was its focus on "active participation" at Mass. We gather as a *community* of God's people. We come not as strangers or rugged individualists or silent spectators. "On the contrary, through a good understanding of the rites and prayers they should take part in the sacred action, conscious of what they are doing, with devotion and full collaboration. They should be instructed by God's word, and be nourished at the table of the Lord's body" (48).

In the time immediately after Vatican Council II there was a lot of turmoil and tension about the changes in the liturgy. People who were schooled one way found it hard to shift gears. To a large extent, however, the turmoil is over. A recent survey of bishops throughout the world shows that Catholics have for the most part responded positively to the new liturgy. While there are a few loud dissenters, the overwhelming majority of people say that they want to learn *more* about the liturgical prayers and actions and join more fully in the celebration. The message of Vatican II has gotten through: the Mass does not "belong" to the priest, but is a treasure of all God's people. The priest has a proper role in the liturgy, one that cannot be delegated to others, but other ministers have proper roles as well: for example, lectors, commentators, servers, choir members or cantors, ushers, and deacons. Many people have found it helpful to *prepare* for the liturgy (for example, by reflecting on the prayers and readings ahead of time) so that they can bring more to it and so derive more from it.

Because the Mass is so important to the life of the Christian community, it is easy to understand why the Church has a serious law obliging us to attend Mass on Sundays and holy days of obligation. To fulfill this obligation, we must attend the *whole* Mass, and we must attend *in person*. (TV Masses are marvelous for people who are sick or shut in, but they are not legitimate substitutes for those who are able to attend in person.) It goes without saying that we should bring as much *devotion* and *attention* as possible to this holy action — and should certainly avoid anything that would render our participation impossible, for example, sleeping or reading a novel. Some distractions are beyond our control and do not invalidate our worship. Saint Alphonsus suggests that in such cases we should simply renew a simple act of faith when we become aware of the distraction, and then go on with our prayer.

While the obligation to take part in Sunday Mass is indeed a serious obligation, serious reasons can excuse a person from attendance. Some examples: sickness, urgent responsibilities of justice or charity (for example, caring for a sick family member), occupation, severe weather, a great distance from a church. While a person should not be troubled in conscience when a serious reason arises, it is also important to make sure that indifference, laziness, or personal pleasure do not masquerade as serious reasons!

Attending Mass faithfully week after week will almost invariably cause some hardship and demand some sacrifice. It is part of the cross which the follower of Christ must expect in his or her life. My experience leads me to believe that the Catholic who is sincerely faithful to Sunday Mass will tend to take the following of Christ seriously. There is a tendency at times to disparage the "Sunday Mass Catholic." The inference seems to be that he or she does "this trivial thing" regularly, but isn't really and truly an involved Christian. Attending Sunday Mass is, to be sure, no guarantee of fidelity to the Lord, but neither is it a trivial thing. The Eucharist is the heart of Catholic worship. The person who is *there* is far better off than the believer who isn't.

The Day of the Lord

Not only is Sunday the day when the Christian community comes together for the celebration of the Eucharist, it is also a special feast day. "The Lord's Day is the original feast day, and it should be proposed to the faithful and taught to them so that it may become in fact a day of joy and freedom from work" *(The Sacred Liturgy,* 106). While the law against "servile work" is in some way connected with the Jewish "Sabbath rest" and in some ways conditioned by historical factors, it still serves some very good purposes.

With his wonderful insight into the faith and into human nature, Pope John XXIII explained why the Sunday rest is still important. First, there is a profoundly *religious* reason: "God has a right to demand of human beings that they dedicate one day of the week to the proper and fitting worship of the eternal Godhead. This should be a day when the spirit is freed from material preoccupations . . . a day when a person can examine the secrets of his conscience and thus grasp the binding force of his sacred relations to his Creator." Without such leisurely freedom, experience testifies, spirituality is easily crowded out by materialism.

Secondly, there is a *family* reason: The observance of Sunday "permits people to promote family unity by making it possible for all the members of the family to enjoy more frequent and harmonious contacts with one another." Many people persist in the illusion that family unity can be strengthened without members of the family spending time together and without intimate sharing. It can't be done.

Finally, there is the *human* need for rest and relaxation: "The human person has the right to and the need of periodic rest. This renews the bodily strength used up by daily work and allows for a decent measure of recreation" *(Christianity and Social Progress).*

Because the Lord's Day is a feast day and because these values are so precious, the present law of the Church states that all servile, judicial, and commercial work is forbidden on Sundays and holy days, but cultural and ordinary work is allowed. Because of the many cultural changes that have occurred in modern societies, it is hard to *define* the terms of this canon and even harder to make applications to real situations. In reflecting on the obligation of Sunday rest, however, we should avoid two extremes.

On the one hand, we should avoid a negative, cheerless, legalistic attitude. Jesus announced the following principle: "The sabbath was made for man, not man for the sabbath" (Mark 2:27). On several occasions Jesus had to challenge the legalistic mentality of the Pharisees who objected to the breaking of the Sabbath regulations. Catholics have not always avoided their own kind of legalism in applying the law against servile work.

On the other hand, we should avoid a careless and completely secular attitude toward the Lord's Day, with the result that it becomes "just another day." I have lived in five states in the last twenty years. Some of them have fairly strict laws about Sunday buying and selling, others have a wide-open policy. I have seen people "fall into the trap" of regular, busy-busy shopping on Sunday for no good reason. In another state the same persons would have gotten along fine without Sunday shopping. A religious attitude and generosity with the Lord are keys in this matter.

Making honest moral decisions in this area can be difficult for many people, especially those of a tender or scrupulous conscience. As a general principle, one might measure his or her decisions against a norm like this: If possible, one should avoid those works and activities which are not compatible with the worship of God or which deprive one of rest and renewal of body and soul. Or, to put it positively, one could say this: If we celebrate the Eucharistic liturgy with reverence and love, if we avoid unnecessary work and business and shopping, if we seek wholesome recreation and fun (especially with our family members), and if we look out for the needs of others (for example, visiting the sick), then we can be quite sure that we are keeping holy the Lord's Day.

CHAPTER SIX
THE QUEST FOR
CHRISTIAN UNITY

"That They All May Be One"

In our day there is another dimension to the virtue of religion that deserves the serious consideration of every Christian: the quest for Christian unity. In the last discourse of Jesus, we hear his urgent prayer: "I do not pray for them alone. I pray also for those who will believe in me through their word, that all may be one as you, Father, are in me, and I in you; I pray that they may be [one] in us, that the world may believe that you sent me. I have given them the glory you gave me that they may be one, as we are one — I living in them, you living in me — that their unity may be complete . . ." (John 17:20-23).

It is a sad fact of history that the Christian Church is a *divided* Church. For many centuries it was not divided: there was a unity of doctrine, a unity of worship, and a unity of organization under the Bishop of Rome. The first great division in the Church did not appear until the eleventh century when a number of Eastern Christians refused to acknowledge the pope as the visible head of the Church. They took the name "Orthodox." They held on to almost all of the Christian teachings; they differ from the Catholic Church mainly on the doctrine of the pope as the Vicar of Christ.

The second major division in the Church, far deeper and wider, came at the time of the Protestant Reformation in the sixteenth century. Under the direction of men like John Calvin and Martin

Luther, new Christian communities grew up in Europe. Fundamental differences about key doctrines of faith began to emerge. Theology became a battleground of argument and counter-argument. Cultural factors also played a large role in the divisions. Through the centuries following the Reformation the divisions seemed to grow. In our day there are a bewildering number of Christian churches and communities.

Early in this century, however, a concerted effort toward Christian unity began to develop. Christian leaders of many churches contributed to this effort, which came to be called "the ecumenical movement." Pope John XXIII was deeply interested in this movement and committed to its growth. In 1959, when he announced his plan to call the Second Vatican Council, he made it clear that he wanted it to give serious attention to Christian unity. He invited observers from other Christian churches to attend the historic Council.

The Council in its turn issued a *Decree on Ecumenism*. This ground-breaking document opened with this statement: "The restoration of unity among all Christians is one of the principal concerns of the Second Vatican Council." The document urged all Catholics to seek Christian unity.

During the years since the Council there have been many efforts toward Christian unity: dialogues at the highest levels of the churches, bringing together bishops, pastors, theologians. But also "living-room dialogues" where ordinary Christians come together to share prayer and to understand one another better.

Truth to tell, however, progress toward Christian unity has been slow. Some of those who started out with such high hopes fifteen years ago, expecting quick results, have become discouraged. In his very first encyclical, Pope John Paul II warned against discouragement. He also chided those who were tempted to give up the quest. "To all who, for whatever motive, would wish to dissuade the Church from seeking the universal unity of Christians, the question must once again be put: Have we the right not to seek it? Can we fail to have trust, in spite of all human weakness and all the faults of past centuries, in our Lord's grace as revealed through what the Holy Spirit said and what we heard during the Council?"

A pregnant sentence in the Council's decree reminded us that "today in many parts of the world, under the inspiring grace of the

Holy Spirit, many efforts are being made in prayer, word and action to attain that fullness of unity which Jesus Christ desires." From this statement, we can take our lead as to what we ourselves can do to foster Christian unity.

The first effort that all of us can make is the effort of *prayer*. Prayer is an absolutely essential condition for Christian unity. There are many occasions when Christians can come together in a spirit of common prayer. For example, there are often occasions of shared prayer at the time of joint meetings, at the time of special holidays such as Thanksgiving and Memorial Day. The Catholic Church also suggests special fixed times when people are encouraged to pray in a special way for Christian unity. The "week of Christian unity" in January is one such time.

The second effort all of us can make is in *word*. First of all, we should speak with great respect for other Christian churches. The Council warns us to "avoid expressions, judgments and actions which do not represent the condition of our separated brethren with truth and fairness and so make mutual relations with them more difficult." It goes without saying that we should also avoid in our conversation any kind of joke or belittling remark about the religion of other people.

In a more positive way, we are encouraged to dialogue with members of other Christian communities. While it is true that experts are consulting with one another at a high level, it is also true that each of us in his or her life can enter into constructive discussions with members of other Christian communities.

The third area in which we can unite our efforts is in the area of *action*. Members of different Christian groups should come together in a united effort to bring the spirit of Christ to the world. There are many concrete ways in which we can join hands to promote family life, to work for social justice, to promote public morality, and to make our neighborhoods reflect more fully the gospel of Jesus Christ.

The quest for Christian unity must go on. All of us must be a part of it. The Lord Jesus, who prayed for unity among his followers, will surely be with us in the quest.

Interfaith Questions

When people are sincerely involved in ecumenical efforts, they will tend to "accentuate the positive and eliminate the negative."

They will strive to pray, work, and dialogue together. Yet at times they also have to face (to complete the phrase from the old song) "Mr. In-Between." That is, they may encounter serious questions about what is and what is not theologically acceptable in interfaith practices.

While one can think of many such questions, two seem to stand out in ordinary pastoral practice. One concerns sharing Eucharistic communion and the other concerns interfaith marriages. That these are questions of fundamental importance is self-evident. They are also extremely complicated. What is said about them in this brief space merely scratches the surface. These remarks, moreover, are from the Catholic viewpoint and do not pretend to do justice to other views.

The sharing of Eucharistic communion must be considered in the light of two general principles. (These principles, and much more besides, can be found in *On Admitting Other Christians to Eucharistic Communion,* by the Secretariat for Promoting Christian Unity, June 1, 1972.) The first principle emphasizes the essential relationship between the mystery of the Church and the mystery of the Eucharist. "Of its very nature celebration of the Eucharist signifies the fullness of profession of faith and the fullness of ecclesial communion. This principle must not be obscured and must remain our guide in the field." We would run the risk of deceiving ourselves if we celebrate a unity of faith that does not yet exist. We must first do the hard work of achieving unity before routinely celebrating it.

The second general principle, however, takes into account the spiritual need of those who wish to approach the Eucharist. The first principle mentioned above "will not be obscured if admission to eucharistic communion is confined to particular cases of those Christians who have faith in the sacrament in conformity with that of the Church, who experience a serious spiritual need of the eucharistic sustenance, who for a prolonged period are unable to have recourse to a minister of their own community, and who ask for the sacrament of their own accord; all this provided that they have proper dispositions and lead lives worthy of a Christian."

While this general principle is clear, many less clear questions can arise about it. The local bishop has been given the authority to judge particular cases. In some dioceses helpful guidelines for particular cases have been published.

One other point should be added. A Catholic in circumstances similar to those outlined above is allowed to ask for the Eucharist only from a minister who has been validly ordained. The reason for this is the faith of the Church that only such a person can consecrate the bread and wine and effect the change of the bread and wine into the Body and Blood of Christ.

It will be a joyful day indeed when the unity of faith among Christians has been achieved and when the Eucharist can be celebrated as a sign of that unity.

Because religion should be a bond of unity in a marriage and not a stumbling block, most churches have frowned on interfaith marriages. The Catholic Church discourages mixed marriages. "There are many difficulties inherent in a mixed marriage, since a certain division is introduced into the living cell of the Church, as the Christian family is rightly called, and in the family itself the fulfillment of the gospel teachings is more difficult because of diversities in matters of religion, especially with regard to those matters which concern Christian worship and the education of the children" (*Apostolic Letter on Mixed Marriages,* January 7, 1970).

Yet most Christian churches today are trying to offer support and help to those couples who intend to enter a mixed marriage. This pastoral approach is certainly preferable to the highly negative approach of some years ago. The Church today directs its attention to the Catholic party, so that he or she will recognize what a serious responsibility it is to preserve his or her faith. It also hopes to inform the non-Catholic party of certain fundamental obligations of the Catholic party, so that these matters will not be a source of turmoil in the marriage.

The Church has formulated some basic guidelines for mixed marriages. Stated flatly, as we must state them here, they may seem anything but ecumenical. In this delicate ecumenical area, we must all try to avoid misunderstandings. The point of these guidelines is to inform and clarify, not to antagonize.

1. A marriage between two baptized persons, of whom one is Catholic and the other non-Catholic, may not *licitly* (lawfully) be contracted without the previous *dispensation* (permission) of the local Ordinary (bishop). The Church is prepared to grant this dispensation for a just cause.

2. To obtain a dispensation, the Catholic party must declare that

he or she is ready to remove dangers of falling away from the faith and will do all in his or her power to have the children baptized and brought up in the Catholic faith. The non-Catholic party must be informed of these promises so that there is no unnecessary confusion. Both parties are also to be instructed on the essential elements of Christian marriage.

3. The *canonical form* of marriage (that is, that the Catholic party be married in the presence of an authorized priest and two witnesses) is necessary for the *validity* of the marriage. The bishop may, however, dispense from this requirement, so that the Catholic party may be married in the non-Catholic Church and before the non-Catholic minister. In such cases a priest may be present at the ceremony and take some part in it (for example, give a reading or a blessing), but he is not to be considered the official witness of the marriage. It should also be noted, since there is some confusion about this, that there is no obligation for the priest to be present. If the couple is married in the Catholic Church, the priest is to be the official witness, welcoming the presence and participation of the non-Catholic minister. The liturgy of the wedding should be worked out with the pastor in whose church the wedding will take place.

4. The entire Christian community should provide encouragement and help to the parties of a mixed marriage, so that they and their children can grow in faith and solve the problems they may encounter.

Other questions can easily arise in this area of life. The couple should not hesitate to seek counsel from their pastors.

PART THREE: LOVE YOUR NEIGHBOR AS YOURSELF

Honor your father and your mother . . .
You shall not kill.
You shall not commit adultery.
You shall not steal.
You shall not bear false witness against your neighbor.
You shall not covet your neighbor's wife . . .
You shall not covet your neighbor's house . . . .

— Book of Exodus

Each family finds within itself a summons that cannot be ignored . . . Family, become what you are!

— Pope John Paul II

Every human life is inviolable from the beginning.

— American Bishops

Sexuality is one of God's greatest gifts to man and woman . . . Chastity is a virtue which liberates the human person.

— Bishop Francis Mugavero

The rule of justice is plain, namely, that a good person ought not to swerve from the truth, not to inflict any unjust loss on anyone, not to act in any way deceitfully.

— Saint Ambrose

Nothing conquers except the truth: the victory of truth is charity.

— Saint Augustine

CHAPTER SEVEN
THE CHRISTIAN FAMILY

Portrait of Christian Marriage

It is easy enough to paint a pessimistic portrait of Christian marriage these days. While comedians joke and sociologists probe, the divorce rates keep rising. The divorce rates are real, to be sure, yet it may be that they distract us from seeing the rest of the picture: namely, that there are many couples who are living the mystery of Christian marriage with great success. It is important that we hear about the breakdown of marriages, but it is equally important that we hear the success stories as well.

Most important of all is that we do not lose sight of what God has revealed to us about marriage. One of the great challenges to the Church in every generation is to wipe away the dust and dirt that cover the portrait, so that its face can shine through. For our generation, the Second Vatican Council has done that.

"The intimate partnership of life and love which constitutes the married state has been established by the creator and endowed by him with its own proper laws: it is rooted in the contract of its partners, that is, in their irrevocable consent. It is an institution confirmed by the divine law and receiving its stability, even in the eyes of society, from the human act by which the partners mutually surrender themselves to each other . . ." (*The Church in the Modern World*, 48).

God is the author of marriage. "The central word of revelation, 'God loves his people,' is likewise proclaimed through the living and concrete word whereby a man and woman express their conjugal love. Their bond of love becomes the image and symbol of the covenant which unites God and his people.'' (The preceding quotation is from *Familiaris Consortio,* 12. This chapter relies heavily on this Apostolic Exhortation of Pope John Paul II, published on December 15, 1981. It is the most complete treatment of the family to come from a papal pen in at least fifty years. In this book it is called simply *Family.*)

Jesus himself blesses and sanctifies the love of husband and wife. ''Just as of old God encountered his people with a covenant of love and fidelity, so our Savior, the spouse of the Church, now encounters Christian spouses through the sacrament of marriage. He abides with them in order that by their mutual self-giving spouses will love each other with enduring fidelity, as he loved the Church and delivered himself for it'' (*The Church in the Modern World,* 48).

Christian marriage is characterized, first of all, by *unity:* ''Thus they are no longer two but one flesh'' (Matthew 19:6). The husband and wife are called to serve and help each other by their married partnership. Each day they become more conscious of their unity and experience it more deeply.

Christian marriage is also characterized by *fidelity. The Church in the Modern World* expresses it this way: ''The intimate union of marriage, as a mutual giving of two persons, and the good of the children demand *total fidelity* of the spouses and require an unbreakable unity between them'' (48).

In his encyclical *Humanae Vitae* (which became widely known because of its teaching on contraception) Pope Paul VI offered a brief but beautiful summary of the *fundamental qualities* of Christian married love. They are surely essential parts of the portrait against which husbands and wives can measure their own love.

First of all, married love is *fully human.* It is of the senses and the spirit at the same time. It embraces body, mind, and soul. It touches every aspect of the couple's life together, the joys and the sorrows of daily life.

Secondly, this love is *total:* that is, it is a very special form of friendship, in which husband and wife generously share everything, without undue reservations or selfish calculations.

Thirdly, married love is *faithful and exclusive* unto death. This fidelity can of course be difficult at times, but it is always possible, always noble, and always meritorious. "The example of so many married persons down through the centuries shows, not only that fidelity is according to the nature of marriage, but also that it is a source of profound and lasting happiness" (*Humanae Vitae*, 9).

Finally, conjugal love is *fruitful*. It is not exhausted by the communion between husband and wife but is open to raise up new lives. Marriage and conjugal love are by their nature ordained toward the begetting and educating of children. Children are the supreme gift of marriage. (Further reflections on Christian marriage and sexuality are found in chapter 9 of this book.)

This portrait of Christian marriage, brief as it is, reminds us of the marvelous plan of God. Because this plan is easily clouded over in our society, and because it is very demanding, the Church is striving with renewed vigor to help couples to *prepare* for marriage and to *live* it.

In almost every diocese in the United States and Canada, one finds a strong emphasis on preparation for marriage. The details vary somewhat (and therefore one's own pastor should be consulted), but the basic aims and procedures are quite similar. It should be stressed that these new policies are not designed as an obstacle to be overcome but rather as a opportunity for reflection and growth. Christian marriage is a lifelong vocation. The engaged couple should be ready and willing to understand as much as possible about the sacrament of marriage and about their own relationship before taking this important step. It is common these days to require that the engaged couple undergo some kind of assessment of their relationship before setting the date. Pre-marriage inventories of one kind or another are filled out by the couple and then evaluated with the help of the priest. Engaged couples are also expected to take part in a formal marriage preparation program, such as Engaged Encounter or Christian Marriage seminars. It is especially heartening to see so many mature married couples sharing their experience and their love in these programs.

But mature married couples need help and encouragement too. A very hopeful "sign of the times" in the Church is the growth of marriage enrichment programs of various kinds. All of these recognize the need that couples have for *time* and *assistance* to deepen their relationship. *Marriage Encounter* has been a Godsend for many couples, because it has helped them to discover new techniques for communication and new ways of expressing their love. There is still an urgent need for more accessible and inexpensive *marriage counseling* for couples who are struggling with difficult problems. The ministry to those preparing for marriage and those already married is one of the most important in the Church today.

Because marriage frequently leads to the establishment of a family, we turn our attention now to some of the basic elements of the Christian family.

Portrait of the Christian Family

Like so many referees, a number of experts seem to be standing over the Christian family ready to count it out. The family has had it, they say; its time of glory is almost over. On the other hand, there are those who grow ecstatic about the new "liberated" family, reaching toward new frontiers of freedom. The freedom is often conceived of, however, as freedom not to be committed to anyone or anything.

Pope John Paul II, looking at both of these extremes, said that "the situation in which the family finds itself presents positive and negative aspects . . . an interplay of light and darkness" (*Family*, 6). The question that poses itself is: How can the family move away from the darkness and more toward the light? The general answer, according to the pope, is by going back to its roots, by seeing with a clear eye what its basic values are, and by striving to incorporate these basic values into its real life. In this context, Pope John Paul II emphasizes *four basic values* of the family.

First, the family is *a community of persons:* husband and wife, parents and children, relatives. The first task of the family is to develop into a real community of persons. How can this be done? Only through *love*. "Without love the family is not a community of persons, and in the same way, without love the family cannot live, grow and perfect itself as a community of persons." With love, on the other hand, the family can grow and reach its full stature. "The love between husband and wife and, in a derivatory and broader way, the love between members of the same family — between parents and children, brothers and sisters, and relatives and members of the household — is given life and sustenance by an unceasing inner dynamism leading the family to ever deeper and more intense communion" (*Family*, 18).

Secondly, *the family is a school of humanity*. Building a community of persons makes demands on all the family members. "All members of the family, each according to his or her own gift, have the grace and the responsibility of building day by day the communion of persons, making the family a school of deeper humanity" (*Family,* 21). In this school, each family member learns to care for others. In the family there will be special care for the young, the sick, the aged. There will be mutual service every day. There will be a sharing of goods and of joys and sorrows. This school obviously requires of each member a generous spirit of sacrifice. Yet it is not the kind of sacrifice that always weighs heavily on one's shoulders. It is the kind that brings happiness and a sense of fulfillment.

Thirdly, *the family is a place of reconciliation*. Wherever people live in close and intimate contact, there will be times of stress and difficulty. Family members can hurt each other in thought, word, and deed. There are many forms of conflict and division in family life. "There is no family that does not know how selfishness, discord, tensions and conflict violently attack and at times mortally wound its own communion: Hence there arise the many and varied forms of division in family life. But, at the same time, every family is called by God of peace to have the joyous and renewing experience of reconciliation, that is communion reestablished, unity restored" (*Family,* 21).

Husbands and wives, particularly, need ongoing reconciliation. Pressured from within and from without, they can easily ignore each other's needs or hurt each other. These small hurts, if not attended to, can fester and become dangerous. A frequent expression of apology or a sincere "I forgive you" can go a long way in a relationship. The ancient advice, "The sun must not go down on your wrath" (Ephesians 4:26), is extremely practical.

Fourthly, *the family is a vital cell of society*. It is in the family that young people learn the values of respect, justice, and love — the very values that are so significant to society. "The family has vital and organic links to society since it is its foundation and nourishes it continually through its role of service to life: It is from the family that citizens come to birth and it is within the family that they find the first school of the social virtues that are the animating principle of the existence and development of society itself" (*Family,* 42).

It is a strange phenomenon, but the values that are most basic to society seem hardly to be prized by the mass media or public education. The family all too often has to struggle *against* the false values instilled in school or by TV. If it weren't for the patient care of parents, where would our social values be? Thus the family promotes authentic social life more effectively than any other single institution.

In addition, it is in the family that the individual, caught up at times in the depersonalized "rat race" of life, can renew his or her personal dignity and experience his or her uniqueness. When family members accept one another "as they are," they help to heal wounds and restore energies and nourish talents. The family member, thus restored, is able to contribute more fully to society as a whole.

This portrait of the Christian family accentuates, to be sure, very high ideals. Families are not perfect and will not attain them all at once. But it is important for Christian families to strive toward these ideals: building community, deepening love, promoting reconciliation, nourishing gifts. It is in such families that happiness and wholeness are found.

Charter of Family Rights

"As the family goes, so goes society." This saying is almost as old as humankind. The strength and vitality of a given society is tied in large measure to the strength and vitality of the families that make it up. To put it in terms of Catholic social philosophy, the family and society are mutually involved in defending and fostering the good of each human person. They have *complimentary* functions.

The ideal of cooperation between the family and society can best be achieved by the principle of *subsidiarity*. This principle says, in effect, that society should let families do for themselves what they are able to do for themselves; but society should come to their aid when they are in need of doing what they are *not* able to do for themselves.

Pope John Paul II explains that "the state cannot and must not take away from families the functions that they can just as well perform on their own or in free associations; instead it must positively favor and encourage as far as possible responsible initiative by families. In the conviction that the good of the family is an indispensable and essential value of the civil community, the public authorities must do everything possible to ensure that families have all those aids — economic, social, educational, political and cultural — that they need in order to face all their responsibilities in a human way" (*Family*, 45).

Unfortunately, this ideal of mutual respect and collaboration is not always present. Harsh separation and even opposition often enough replace the ideal. With stinging accuracy the pope asserts: "Institutions and laws unjustly ignore the inviolable rights of the family and of the human person; and society, far from putting itself at the service of the family, attacks it violently in its values and fundamental needs. Thus, the family . . . finds itself the victim of society, of the delays and slowness with which it acts, and even of its blatant injustice" (*Family*, 46).

When the synod of bishops met in 1981 to discuss the needs and problems of the family, bishops from all over the world offered many important suggestions. Pope John Paul II gathered these suggestions together, refined them, and issued this "charter of family rights":

- The right to exist and progress as a family, that is, the right of every human being, even if he or she is poor, to found a family and to have adequate means to support it.
- The right to exercise its responsibility regarding the transmission of life and to educate children.
- The right to the intimacy of conjugal and family life.
- The right to the stability of the bond and the institution of marriage.
- The right to believe in and profess one's faith and to propagate it.
- The right to bring up children in accord with the family's own traditions and religious values, with the necessary instruments, means, and institutions.
- The right, especially of the poor and sick, to obtain physical, social, political, and economic security.
- The right to housing suitable for living family life in a suitable way.
- The right to expression and representation, either directly or through associations, before the economic, social, and cultural public authorities.

- The right to form associations with other families and institutions in order to fulfill the family's role suitably.
- The right to protect minors by adequate legislation from harmful drugs, pornography, alcoholism, etc.
- The right to wholesome recreation of a kind that also fosters family values.
- The right of the elderly to a worthy life and a worthy death.
- The right to emigrate as a family in search of a better life.

While this charter of family rights may strike some people as an impossible Utopia, no one can deny that a healthy society needs healthy families. Every society should place the *highest priority* on the needs of the family. Each citizen should support the kinds of legislation and programs that will help, not destroy, the family unit. Obviously, there is room for disagreement about the best means to help the family, and that's where politics comes in. But the goal is a moral imperative which every Christian should take seriously.

Since the family is made up of individual members who have various roles and functions to fulfill, we turn our attention at this point to the key players: father, mother, children.

The Role of Husband and Father

It is not easy to talk about the role of husband and father in the Christian family. The ghost of the past hovers over our discussions: the patriarch of the patriarchal family! Many people have disowned this ogre and shy away from reviving him in any shape or form. Yet the role of husband and father remains crucial. It is, to be sure, a demanding role, calling for a great deal of unselfish love and sacrifice. When generously fulfilled, however, it brings the kind of joy and satisfaction a man may find nowhere else.

For the majority of people, the relationship between husband and wife is the most intimate relationship they will ever experience. It is a relationship deeply rooted in human nature as designed by God: "It is not good for the man to be alone. I will make a suitable partner for him" (Genesis 2:18). The first husband, Adam, expressed his delight and appreciation for the gift of his wife: "This one, at last, is bone of my bones and flesh of my flesh" (Genesis 2:23).

According to the Christian tradition at its best, the relationship of a husband to his wife should rest on the solid foundation of two pillars: equality and love. It must be granted that in the long course of Christian history this tradition has not always been observed. Experience seems to prove, however, that when these pillars are absent, the relationship will crumble. When they are present, the relationship will "stand strong and fine, like a mountain pine."

First, *equality*. Against many cultural and social odds, a husband must have a profound personal respect for his wife and for her equal dignity. Writing in the fifth century, Saint Ambrose summarized the best of the tradition when he said to Christian husbands: "You are not your wife's master, but her husband; she was not given to you to be your slave, but your wife . . . Reciprocate her attentiveness to you and be grateful to her for her love." That admonition is as wise today, and as needed, as it was in the fifth century.

Second, *love*. The Christian husband is called to develop a new attitude of love toward his wife. In the words of Saint Paul, which startle no matter how often they are heard, he is called to love his wife as Christ loves the Church. "Husbands, love your wives, as Christ loved the Church. He gave himself up for her . . ." (Ephesians 5:25). This authentic love involves, as we noted earlier, a special kind of friendship, a generous sharing of everything, a tireless commitment "in good times and in bad."

When a husband and wife are blessed with children, the husband is called to the new role of fatherhood. It is in itself a demanding role. It becomes more so in a cultural atmosphere which tends to downplay the unique role of the father as nurturer and educator of his children. For at least twenty-five years, TV sit-coms have made dad the boob of the tube. Like water pounding on a rock, the cultural pounding has had its subtle influence on both fathers and children.

The first condition for fatherhood is *presence*. Both experience and research show that the absence of the father "causes psychological and moral imbalance and notable difficulties in family relationships." If the absence is due to death, family members seem able to adjust to it. But when it is due to voluntary abandonment, the scars remain unhealed a long, long time.

Presence alone, however, is not enough. For there can be, in the strong words of John Paul II, "the *oppressive* presence of a father, especially where there still prevails the phenomenon of 'machismo,' or a wrong superiority of male prerogatives which humiliates women and inhibits the development of healthy family relationships'' (*Family*, 25).

The kind of presence that is necessary is a loving and caring presence, one that reflects the very fatherhood of God. This means that the father tries to be generous and unselfish in meeting the needs of all the members of the family. He puts his family first, careful that his work and his outside commitments do not cause division and discord among the people he loves most. If there is a single complaint that ranks as number one among wives and children, it is that the husband and father doesn't spend enough time with them. The reasons for this may seem quite important to the man, but it remains a matter of letting important things rob one of the best things.

In addition to presence, the father must *participate* with his wife in the challenge of educating the children. There is no substitute for his contribution to their growth and development. The philosophy that wants to leave ''all that'' to the mother alone is a misguided one. It deprives the children of a splendid and irreplaceable gift and makes the father poorer as well.

Finally, he strives to be a living example of an adult Christian. He takes his faith seriously, practices it faithfully, and passes on to his children the great heritage which he has received. Spiritual leadership is not a matter of ranting and raving but of faithful discipleship, of actions which speak louder than words. Blessed are those children who have a father who practices what he preaches!

The Role of Wife and Mother

If it is difficult to talk about the role of husband and father in the Christian family, it is perhaps even more difficult, amid the cultural challenges on all sides, to speak of the role of wife and mother. No one doubts that the role is a demanding one. It is also a supremely important one.

God created the human person in his own image and likeness and called each person to a life of love. In the striking sentence of Pope John Paul II, ''Love is the fundamental and innate vocation of every human being.'' But that vocation to love must be expressed in a concrete way of life. For the majority of people, that way of life is marriage.

Christian marriage is certainly a vocation to love. It can be defined as "a covenant of love" between wife and husband. The Church does not hesitate to teach that "the marriage of the baptized becomes a real symbol of that new and eternal covenant sanctioned by the blood of Christ. The spirit which the Lord pours forth gives a new heart, and renders man and woman capable of loving one another as Christ has loved us" (*Family,* 13).

The Christian wife, then, is called to love her husband with generous love. It is the kind of love about which Saint Paul speaks in his famous hymn to love: "Love is patient; love is kind. Love is not jealous, it does not put on airs, it is not snobbish. Love is never rude, it is not self-seeking, it is not prone to anger; neither does it brood over injuries" (1 Corinthians 13:4-5).

At first blush, considering the downward pull of human nature, it seems impossible to achieve that kind of love. Perhaps it is *humanly* impossible. But with the Lord's abiding grace it is definitely possible. "My grace is enough for you, for in weakness power reaches perfection" (2 Corinthians 12:9). In the Catholic tradition, marriage is a sacrament. In part, that signifies that the married person receives all the graces necessary to achieve the purpose of the sacrament. This "sacramental grace" helps the Christian wife grow toward a generous, tender, self-giving love for her husband.

It need hardly be added that the role of mother also signifies a vocation to love. There is an ever-present temptation to sentimentalize or "sugarize" mother love. But real mother love is not at all weak or trivial. On the contrary, it is deep and strong and wise and lasting.

The love of a mother for her child has many dimensions. It seems to me that two basic characteristics stand out. First, *mother love strives to be unconditional*. This is the kind of love with which Christ loves us. In the description of John Powell, S.J., Jesus says to us: "You have my love. You don't have to pay for it. You didn't earn it and you can't deserve it. You only have to open up to it and receive it" (*Free to Be Me,* 20).

The only kind of love that makes a difference in another's life is unconditional love. As we know from experience, unconditional love is scarce in life. Blessed is the child who receives it from a parent! "If people are loved because they are pretty or get good marks in school, because they keep their clothes clean or become good athletes, in the end they don't feel loved at all," adds Father Powell (*Free to Be Me*, 12). Without doubt, the greatest gift a mother can give a child is the gift of unconditional love. For that gift she will be long remembered.

Secondly, however, *mother love is also challenging*. The young person who has experienced unconditional love is better able to accept "tough love." Most people do not really use all of their gifts and talents. They must be challenged to do so. This is especially true of growing children. A mother who truly loves her child is in the best possible position to challenge him or her. It is, in truth, a great service of love.

The role of wife and mother, never easy, is even more difficult today as women struggle with legitimate feminist aspirations and confront the larger society. That "many forms of degrading discrimination" against women still persist in our society (in the areas of employment, wages, and education particularly) is beyond dispute. Women are of course the first victims. But the rest of us are victims as well. The 1981 synod of bishops deplored all such forms of discrimination and called upon all of us to help overcome them "so that the image of God that shines in all human beings without exception may be fully respected" (*Family*, 24).

Children: Rights and Responsibilities

It was Jesus himself who declared the importance of children in the kingdom of God: "Let the little children come to me. Do not shut them off. The reign of God belongs to such as these. Trust me when I tell you that whoever does not accept the kingdom of God as a child will not enter into it" (Luke 18:16).

The Second Vatican Council summarized a long tradition of Christian conviction when it said: "Marriage and married love are by nature ordered to the procreation and education of children. Indeed children are the supreme gift of marriage and greatly contribute to the good of parents themselves" (*Church in the Modern World*, 50).

Experience shows, however, that it is easier to wax eloquent about children than it is to take care of their basic needs and preserve their basic rights. In these days of child abuse and neglect, Pope John Paul II emphasizes that "special attention must be devoted to children by developing a profound esteem for their personal dignity and a great respect and generous concern for their rights. This is true for every child, but it becomes all the more urgent the smaller the child is and the more it is in need of everything, when it is sick, suffering or handicapped'' (*Family,* 26).

Concern for the child, from the first moment of conception and throughout the years of infancy and youth, is the characteristic mark of the Christian community and a humane society. Whatever is done to foster and nourish the health, education, and spiritual growth of children is a contribution to the present and future of civilization and the Church.

Yet children are not only ''receivers'' in the family, they are also called to be ''givers.'' What do children give to their parents? What contribution do they make to the family?

The fourth commandment states: ''Honor your father and your mother, that you may have a long life in the land which the Lord, your God, is giving you'' (Exodus 20:12). Jesus repeated this commandment to the rich young man (Matthew 19:19) and Paul in his turn spelled it out for the Ephesians (6:2).

What does the ''honor'' of this commandment signify? Moralists suggest that, by force of this commandment, children must show to their parents reverence, love, and obedience. A brief word about each of these.

Reverence: Parents are cooperators with God in giving children the gift of life. They take God's place in the child's life. This is not to say that parents are ''gods'' or even that they always act justly and lovingly. But they do have a specific role to play in the child's life, and that role deserves respect. Reverence means seeking what is for the welfare of parents, taking care of them in their needs. It means not talking back to them in an angry way, not belittling them, not acting defiantly toward them.

Love: To love one's parents means to foster their spiritual and material welfare, to do what will make them happy, to pray for them. It means helping them by sharing the burdens of family life and doing the chores that must be done. It means trying to develop a spirit of cooperation and good will in the family, not a spirit of dissension and argument. It means showing our parents signs of affection in word and deed.

Obedience: ''You children, obey your parents in everything, for that is the acceptable way in the Lord'' (Colossians 3:20). Obedience is a practical expression of love. It means accepting the directions of parents and abiding by their decisions. It means fulfilling their commands for the total welfare of the family. It means making practical contributions to the common good of the family.

There is no time limit on the reverence and love a child owes his or her parents. Reverence and love should follow our parents to their graves. There *is* a limit to the obedience a child owes his or her parents. The obligation ends when a child is no longer under the authority of his or her parents (has reached his or her majority) or has definitively left home. At any age, however, the person who is still living at home should cooperate with the rules that are set down for the good of the parents and other members of the family.

Divorce and the Family

Like the physical plagues of old, descending quietly and soon raging into epidemic proportions, the social plague of divorce has in a short time become a modern-day epidemic. There are over one million divorces a year in the United States. Father Medard Laz says that ''one out of every five people in our country is presently separated or divorced, once was separated or divorced, or has come from a home disrupted by separation or divorce'' *(Helps for the Separated and Divorced)*. Nearly one-third of all school-age children are *not* living with both natural parents.

The frequency of divorce does not take away the agony of it. Divorce seems almost always a matter of immeasurable sadness. It affects the spouses in very deep and personal ways. In my pastoral experience, I felt that divorce had an especially devastating effect on Catholic men and women. It involved not only a failure of human love for which there was once high hopes but also, somehow, a failure of faith. Divorce affects children in many ways, almost all of them painful. On younger children its effect is in a real sense incalculable.

While the epidemic of divorce has been spreading in the Western world, the Catholic Church's teaching on the indissolubility of marriage has remained constant. Some people imply that this is due to an unrealistic traditionalism, but in all fairness it must be said that it is due to the Church's understanding of the teaching of Jesus.

"Then some Pharisees came up and as a test began to ask him whether it was permissible for a husband to divorce his wife. In reply he said, 'What command did Moses give you?' They answered, 'Moses permitted divorce and the writing of a decree of divorce.' But Jesus told them: 'He wrote that commandment for you because of your stubbornness. At the beginning of creation God made them male and female; for this reason a man shall leave his father and mother and the two shall become as one. They are no longer two but one flesh. Therefore let no man separate what God has joined.' Back in the house again, the disciples began to question him about this. He told them, 'Whoever divorces his wife and marries another commits adultery against her; and the woman who divorces her husband and marries another commits adultery' " (Mark 10:2-12).

The Church believes that Jesus' condemnation of divorce in this and other texts is absolute and unqualified. "It is a fundamental duty of the Church to reaffirm strongly, as the synod fathers did, the doctrine of the indissolubility of marriage . . . The gift of the sacrament of Matrimony is at the same time a vocation and a commandment for the Christian spouses, that they may remain faithful to each other forever, beyond every trial and difficulty, in generous obedience to the holy will of the Lord: 'What therefore God has joined together, let no man put asunder' " (*Family,* 20).

Yet, while the Church proclaims the teaching of Christ, a growing number of her sons and daughters are in fact divorced and in some cases remarried as well. This creates a classic dilemma for the Church. It is thus described by the American bishops: "It remains a tragic fact that some marriages fail. We must approach those who suffer this agonizing experience with the compassion of Jesus himself. In some cases romanticism or immaturity may have prevented them from entering into real Christian marriages. But often enough 'broken marriages' are sacramental, indissoluble unions. In this sensitive area the pastoral response of the Church is especially needed and especially difficult to formulate" (*To Live in Christ Jesus,* 16).

The pastoral response of the Church has been developing along several lines. First of all, *there is a growing ministry to divorced and separated Catholics.* Many priests and religious, as well as divorced men and women, are involved in this ministry. It includes spiritual guidance and personal support, conferences and study groups, the exchange of feelings and experiences, tips on practical points, and the like. This ministry has many forms and goes by many names. A divorced person can usually obtain information about what is available in his or her diocese by calling the Chancery Office or one's own parish.

Pope John Paul II recently called upon "pastors and the whole community of the faithful to help the divorced and with solicitous care to make sure that they do not consider themselves as separated from the Church, for as baptized persons they can and indeed must share in her life" (*Family*, 84).

One of the questions that frequently arises is the question of divorced persons receiving the Eucharist. Here we must carefully distinguish two cases.

1) Those Catholics who are *divorced but not remarried* may continue to receive the sacraments and participate fully in the life of the Church. Such people need the support of the Church community more than ever, and there is no reason they should not have it.

2) Those Catholics who are *divorced and remarried* may not be admitted to the Eucharist. Pope John Paul II wrote in 1981: "The Church reaffirms her practice, which is based upon sacred scripture, of not admitting to eucharistic communion divorced persons who have remarried. They are unable to be admitted thereto from the fact that their state and condition of life objectively contradict that union of love between Christ and the Church which is signified and effected by the Eucharist" (*Family*, 84). At the same time the pope encouraged these people "to listen to the word of God, to attend the sacrifice of the Mass, to persevere in prayer, to contribute to works of charity and to community efforts in favor of justice, to bring up their children in the Christian faith, to cultivate the spirit and practice of penance and thus implore, day by day, God's grace."

Part of the Church's ministry to the divorced involves *the annulment process*. A complete treatment of this matter is beyond the scope of these pages, but a few clarifying remarks may be helpful. An annulment is a declaration by the Church that a man and woman *never entered into a true Christian marriage*. The Church arrives at such a decision only after careful investigation. This investigation is carried out by *the matrimonial tribunal* of the diocese.

The Church has certain presumptions in favor of marriage. The Church *presumes* that two baptized Christians who exchange marriage vows and consummate their union have entered into a sacramental marriage which cannot be dissolved by any power on earth, including the Church itself. That presumption yields to fact, however, and if there is clear evidence that an essential ingredient for a true Christian marriage was lacking, then the matrimonial tribunal can declare that a sacramental bond never existed in the first place.

The annulment process takes time. Information must be gathered, witnesses interviewed, details checked. Any priest can help a Catholic *start* the process. The process is then carried out by the diocesan matrimonial tribunal. It is not possible to say exactly how long the process will take, since that depends on many factors. Nor is it possible to state here how much the individual will be asked to contribute toward the cost of processing the annulment. This varies in accord with the circumstances of different dioceses. More accurate information about time and cost can be obtained at the local level.

It is sometimes said, with a touch of cynicism, that an annulment is the Church's form of divorce. In truth, the Church's process reflects a caring attitude toward the faithful and a desire to arrive at the truth. The Church strives on the one hand to uphold the sanctity and indissolubility of Christian marriage, and on the other to give "broken marriages" a fair and just review.

CHAPTER EIGHT
QUESTIONS ABOUT LIFE
AND DEATH

Life Is a Gift of God

In the Christian view of life, God is the Giver of every gift. "Make no mistake about this . . . Every worthwhile gift, every genuine benefit comes from above, descending from the Father of the heavenly luminaries, who cannot change and who is never shadowed over" (James 1:17).

The most basic gift of all is the gift of life itself. "Human life is the basis of all good and is the necessary source and condition of every human activity and of all society. Most people regard life as something sacred and hold that no one may dispose of it at will, but believers see in life something greater, namely a gift of God's love which they are called upon to preserve and make fruitful." (This quotation is taken from the *Declaration on Euthanasia* of the Congregation for the Doctrine of the Faith, June 1980. This very helpful document will be cited a number of times in this chapter under the title *Euthanasia*. There are no paragraph numbers in the original, probably because the document is relatively short.)

God's supremacy over human life is touchingly expressed by the mother of seven sons, all of whom she exhorted in this way: "I do not know how you came into existence in my womb; it was not I who gave you the breath of life, nor was it I who set in order the elements of which each of you is composed. Therefore, since it is the Creator of the universe who shapes each man's beginning, as he brings about the origin of everything, he, in his mercy, will give you back both breath and life . . .'' (2 Maccabees 7:22-23). The faith of the Church is that God is the Creator of human life and that he alone has absolute mastery over it.

Because life is a gift of God, the Christian cherishes it, guards and protects it. Our responsibilities on behalf of life are often considered under the umbrella of ''stewardship'': that is, that the human person is not the absolute master of life and health but, rather, the ''steward'' or ''trustee'' of them. God's gifts are ''on loan'' or ''in trust'' to us. Made in the image and likeness of God, we are called to be ''good stewards'' of our own life and that of others.

In light of the tremendous value of human life, certain basic moral positions must be strongly maintained. The fifth commandment, ''You shall not kill,'' is designed by God for the protection of human life. There are many ways of violating this commandment. Here we want to examine some of the more serious ways.

1. *Murder.* Here we refer to *the unjust killing of an innocent human being.* This is obviously a most serious attack on the rights of God over human life. To take the life of an innocent human person is to commit a sin that cries to heaven for vengeance. (See Genesis 4:10.) Catholic moral teaching is clearly expressed in this principle: ''No one can make an attempt on the life of an innocent person without opposing God's love for that person, without violating a fundamental right and, therefore, without committing a crime of the utmost gravity'' *(Euthanasia).*

2. *Abortion:* Here we refer to *the deliberate destruction of the fetus in the womb.* It is utterly important that we recognize the true meaning of abortion. The unborn child is not simply a mass of matter, not simply an ''appendage'' of the mother. The unborn child is a human person made in the image and likeness of God. He or she has the *right* to life. To take life away from this helpless and defenseless person is, in a word, murder.

The legalization of abortion in the United States in 1973 has led to the criminal mentality of abortion-on-demand. That such a mentality can exist in a civilized and humane society is incredible to me. Because abortion is so widespread, it is possible for unsophisticated people (especially the young) to fall into the trap of considering it normal. The American bishops have expressed the profound immorality of abortion in clear terms: "Every human life is inviolable from its very beginning. While the unborn child may not be aware of itself and its rights, it is a human entity, a human being with potential, not a potential human being. Like the newborn, the unborn depend on others for life and the opportunity to share human goods . . . To destroy these innocent unborn children is *an unspeakable crime*, a crime which subordinates weaker members of the human community to the interests of the stronger . . . Their right to life must be recognized and fully protected by the law" (*To Live in Christ Jesus*, 23).

Fortunately for our society, there are a growing number of people who are taking a stand *in favor of life*. These pro-life or right-to-life groups deserve the participation and collaboration of every American citizen who cares deeply about our society. Only by a strong and persevering effort against present abortion policy can we hope to maintain the basic justice and compassion on which this nation was built. In addition, all of us must pool our efforts to reach out in loving responsibility to those women who see abortion as a solution to agonizing problems. "The Church must take appropriate initiatives in providing support to women with problems during pregnancy or after, and in doing so bear witness to its belief in human dignity" (*To Live in Christ Jesus*, 23). Most dioceses have set up centers for information, counseling, and assistance. One can obtain local information by approaching one's pastor or the Family Life Services of the diocese.

3. *Euthanasia*. Here we refer to *the deliberate killing of persons who are terminally ill or deeply impaired*. "By euthanasia is understood an action or an omission which of itself or by intention causes death, in order that all suffering may in this way be eliminated" (*Euthanasia*). Such "mercy killing" is clearly incompatible with respect for human dignity and reverence for the sacredness of human life.

In this case, as in the case of abortion, words and concepts are used so loosely and falsely that we may be deceived into an erroneous moral evaluation. Catholic teaching on euthanasia goes to the heart of the matter: "It is necessary to state once more that nothing and no one can in any way permit the killing of an innocent human being, whether a fetus or an embryo, an infant or an adult, an older person, or one suffering from an incurable disease or a person who is dying. Furthermore, no one is permitted to ask for this act of killing, either for himself or herself or for another person entrusted to his or her care, nor can he or she consent to it, either explicitly or implicitly. Nor can any authority legitimately recommend or permit such action. For it is a question of the divine law, an offense against the dignity of the human person, a crime against life, and an attack on humanity" (*Euthanasia*).

This comprehensive statement spells out what we mean when we say that "every human life is inviolable from its beginning." The Church, the community of believers, is at its very best when it promotes and defends human life at every stage. "Against the pessimism and selfishness which cast a shadow over the world, the church stands for life: In each human life she sees the splendor of that 'yes,' that 'amen,' who is Christ himself. To the 'no' which assails and afflicts the world, she replies with this living 'yes,' thus defending the human person and the world from all who plot against and harm life" (*Family*, 30).

When It's Time to Die

There is a short phrase that deserves our serious attention. It is sometimes used by those who favor euthanasia (as defined above) and also by those who oppose it. The phrase is: "the right to die with dignity."

Morally speaking, what does this phrase mean? As we have seen, it cannot mean the right to procure death either by one's own hand or by means of someone else. Rather, it means the right to die peacefully and naturally, with human and Christian dignity.

There is a very important distinction here. Some people fail to distinguish between "the direct killing of the innocent who are suffering" and "respecting the dying process." From a moral viewpoint, there is all the difference in the world! Direct killing is gravely wrong. But it does not follow that there is an obligation to *prolong* life by every available means. There comes a time when "letting a person die" is an authentic Christian way of acting.

Many complex situations arise in which there is tension between the use of medical means and the application of moral norms. A growing number of individuals and families have to face these agonizing situations. It will be helpful, therefore, to examine the following question: What moral principles must guide us in making these decisions?

We can start with the following *general moral principle:* "It will be possible to make a correct judgment as to means, by studying the type of treatment to be used, its degree of complexity or risk, its cost and the possibilities of using it, and comparing these elements with the result that can be expected, taking into account the state of the sick person and his or her physical and moral resources" *(Euthanasia).*

Like a suitcase ready for summer vacation, there is a lot packed into that principle! The *Declaration on Euthanasia* helps us to "un-pack" it by the following clarifications:

(a) If there are no other sufficient remedies, it is permissible, with the patient's consent, to use the most advanced medical techniques, even if these are at the *experimental* stage and not without a certain risk.

(b) It is also permitted, with the patient's consent, *to interrupt these means,* where the results fall short of expectations. Before such a decision is made, the reasonable wishes of the patient's *family* should be considered and also the advice of competent doctors. They may judge that the investment in medical instruments and personnel is *disproportionate* to the results foreseen. Or they may judge that the techniques applied impose on the patient suffering *out of proportion* to the benefits which he or she may gain from such techniques.

(c) It is permissible to make do with the *normal means* that medicine can offer. Therefore, one *cannot impose* on anyone the obligation to have recourse to a technique which is in use but which carries a risk or burden with it. Such a refusal is *not* the equivalent of suicide.

(d) When inevitable death is imminent in spite of the means used, it is permitted in conscience to *refuse* forms of treatment that would only secure a prolongation of life, so long as the normal care due to the sick person is not interrupted. In such circumstances the doctor has no reason to reproach himself with failing to help the person in danger.

These principles refer several times to medical procedures or techniques that are *disproportionate* to the results that can be reasonably hoped for. Another way of describing these disproportionate means is to call them "extraordinary means." Perhaps we can draw out some of the implications of these principles by looking at some of the concrete factors that come into play and by giving some commonplace examples. Three factors that must be considered in most cases would be: excessive expense, excessive pain, excessive danger.

(1) *Excessive expense.* Most of us would want to believe that money should not be an obstacle to rescuing or supporting the life of a human being. Yet we know that it can be. In this regard, we cannot lay down any absolute sum of money and say that that is extraordinary or disproportionate. We must take into account the relative financial condition of the person and his or her family. If the expense would involve a grave hardship for the individual or family, the individual would not be obliged to undergo the treatment. For example, if a man would have to spend $35,000 a year to maintain the life of his wife who was afflicted with irreversible brain damage, and in so doing would have to go deep in debt, thus jeopardizing his own future and that of his children, the cost would soon make her medical care a disproportionate or extraordinary means of preserving life.

(2) *Excessive pain.* Obviously, this factor depends very much on circumstances. In our society, where anesthetics are routine, the measure of pain itself will not usually render an operation or technique extraordinary. However, for some people their psychological state of mind makes a terror of all surgery; others can sustain pain over a long period of time; for some, suffering may have a positive moral and spiritual value; for still others, the strain and depression involved in seeing one's life become an extension of a machine (such as the "kidney machine") can make that procedure an extraordinary means.

(3) *Excessive danger.* Here we refer to the "hope of success." This is an extremely important factor. No one is bound to adopt useless measures to preserve his or her life. If an operation or treatment does not carry with it a reasonable assurance that the person will enjoy the benefit of a worthwhile period of time, the treatment is extraordinary. Thus, for example, a person dying of cancer would not have to undergo a major operation which would prolong life for a few months at best.

The serious moral principles which we have been considering in this chapter are at times hard to grasp and at times extremely hard to apply in practice. Some years ago I came across a short statement that summarized for the average person what we have been saying here. It is a positive and joyous statement and deserves our attention. It was published in 1974 by the Catholic Health Association of the United States. It is not to be considered a legal document but a document for reflection and meditation, which can help inform loved ones and physicians how a patient feels about medical treatment at the time of terminal illness.

Christian Affirmation of Life

I, _____, request that I be informed as death approaches so that I may continue to prepare for the full encounter with Christ through the help of the sacraments and the consolation and prayers of my family and friends. I request that, if possible, I be consulted concerning the medical procedures which might be used to prolong life as death approaches. If I can no longer take part in decisions concerning my own future and there is no reasonable expectation of my recovery from physical and mental disability, I request that no extraordinary means be used to prolong my life.

I request, though I wish to join my suffering to the suffering of Jesus so I may be united with him in the act of death-resurrection, that my pain, if unbearable, be alleviated. However, no means should be used with the intention of shortening my life.

I request, because I am a sinner and in need of reconciliation and because my faith, hope, and love may not overcome all fear and doubt, that my family, my friends, and the whole Christian community join me in prayer and mortification as I prepare for the great personal act of dying.

Finally, I request that after my death, my family, my friends, and the whole Christian community pray for me, and rejoice with me because of the mercy and love of the Trinity, with whom I hope to be united for all eternity.

Stewardship of Life and Health

Because life is such a great gift of God, each person has the corresponding responsibility to cherish and protect it. Objectively speaking, the greatest failure of stewardship over life is *suicide*.

"Intentionally causing one's own death, or suicide, is equally as wrong as murder. Such an action on the part of a person is to be considered as a rejection of God's sovereignty and loving plan. Furthermore, suicide is also often a refusal of love for self, the denial of the natural instinct to live, a flight from the duties of justice and charity owed to others" *(Euthanasia)*.

Yet both research and experience tell us that most suicides are due to profound psychological disturbances or mental imbalances. People get caught in such tight and narrow binds that they see suicide as the only way out. On the face of it, suicide is indeed a serious violation of God's law. Yet we must be careful not to judge those who commit suicide. Psychological pressures can be so oppressive as to diminish moral responsibility or even completely remove it. Present law of the Church denies Christian burial to those who have committed suicide, but only if the act was *deliberate*. Psychological disturbance is ordinarily presumed.

While suicide is obviously a failure of stewardship in the most serious way possible, there are many *other* dimensions to stewardship and many moral questions as well. In the Catholic tradition, there is a basic moral principle that can be stated in this way: *The human person has a moral responsibility to take reasonable care of his or her health*. To attempt an exact definition of health would take us far afield, but it is safe to say that health here refers to the "holistic" concept: the care of and harmony between one's physical, mental, and spiritual capacities.

It is, of course, impossible to offer an exact list of all the things demanded by this moral principle. It includes one's responsibility to maintain a balanced diet, take adequate exercise, achieve a proper blend of work and rest and recreation, control tension and stress, and other such reasonable steps. Good stewardship also includes the seeking of competent medical help and the responsible use of ordinary medical procedures and medications when professionally prescribed.

At the same time, however, the Christian person fully realizes that bodily life cannot go on forever. Nor is it the one and only good worth preserving! There can be a *cult* of bodily care which attaches excessive importance to physical health and well-being. The true Christian tries to avoid this cult, while at the same time avoiding the opposite extreme. To oversimplify, the Christian stance may be described by a "do" and a "don't." *Do* everything reasonable to promote good health. *Don't* do those things that are likely to harm or ruin it.

Many particular ethical questions arise in health care. These are usually treated in "medical ethics" or "health care ethics." Here we will touch briefly on some of the more important questions.

1. *Mutilation* is the destruction of some member or function of the body. Stewardship implies that we do not have the right to allow mutilation at will but only when it is necessary for the good of the whole. To sacrifice "a part for the sake of the whole" is often referred to as "the principle of totality" and was thus described by Pope Pius XII: "Each of the bodily organs and members can be sacrificed if it puts the whole organism in danger, a danger which cannot in any other way be averted" (*Address to Roman Guild of St. Luke,* 1944).

By virtue of this principle, Catholic moralists would ordinarily raise no moral objection to the removal of diseased organs, the removal of healthy organs when medically indicated to preserve the well-being of the whole body, blood transfusions, plastic surgery, skin and bone grafts and the like.

2. *Organ Transplants.* Two types of organ transplants are possible. *One* involves an organ or tissue taken from a dead person and given to a living person, for example, a heart transplant. There is no moral problem with this type of transplant, provided, of course, the donor is truly dead. Nor is there any objection to a person donating his or her organs for transplant use after his or her death. Pope Pius XII said that this was positively justified and could be a great act of charity.

A *second* type of transplant involves an organ taken from a living person and given to another living person (for example, kidney transplant). There are some problems here, such as the unavoidable disability left in the person from whom the organ is taken and the general risk to his or her own health. Provided that the living donor has given his or her free and informed consent and provided that the medical indications are positive, this kind of transplant may be justified on the basis of charity toward one's neighbor. The following norm expresses the Catholic position: "The transplantation of organs from living donors is morally permissible when the anticipated benefit to the recipient is proportionate to the harm done to the donor, provided that the loss of such organ(s) does not deprive the donor of life itself nor of the functional integrity of his body" *(The Ethical and Religious Directives for Catholic Health Facilities,* 30).

3. *Sterilization.* Sterilization is depriving a person of the reproductive function. Like other mutilations, it is morally justified when necessary for life or health (for example, the removal of a cancerous uterus). As a contraceptive measure, however, it is considered a grave violation of the moral law. We will take a closer look at the Church's teaching on contraception in the next chapter. Suffice it to say here that, according to the teaching of Pope Paul VI in *Humanae Vitae,* "direct sterilization, whether permanent or temporary, whether of the man or the woman" is to be absolutely excluded as a licit means of regulating birth.

4. *Use of Drugs.* Stewardship of life and health demands that we examine the use of drugs. In this extremely complicated area of modern life and morality, we cannot hope to do justice to the subject in these pages. But perhaps we can establish a moral framework in which the use of drugs can be judged.

Psychotropic (or psychoactive) drugs are chemicals that influence the working of the mind and alter behavior, mood, and mental functioning. These drugs may be distinguished into two main categories: *therapeutic* and *nontherapeutic.*

Therapeutic drugs fall into three main categories: (a) *antipsychotic* drugs are used to treat major mental illnesses such as schizophrenia and paranoia by suppressing the symptoms and helping the person to cope — these are often called *major* tranquilizers; (b) *antidepressant* drugs stimulate the central nervous system and provide relief for depression; (c) *antianxiety* drugs are used to combat anxiety and tension — these are often called the *minor* tranquilizers (including Valium, which is said to be the most prescribed drug in the whole world).

The use of therapeutic drugs is considered morally justified provided they are used under the direction of a competent physician and are believed to be for the total good of the patient. Yet many urgent moral questions must be raised about the use of drugs in our society. It is important that the side effects and the long-range effects be carefully considered and weighed. It is also important that the free consent of the patient (or proxy) be given.

Benedict M. Ashley, O.P., and Kevin D. O'Rourke, O.P., pinpoint some of the questions that must be evaluated: "Simply because a particular therapy alleviates or eliminates a symptom does not mean that it is ethically acceptable. Most of the drugs currently available for the relief of anxiety and tension carry some danger of dependency, habituation, and addiction. Such dependency diminishes human freedom and dignity and hence must be avoided. Thus, the very theory prevalent in our country of using psychoactive drugs to treat psychological difficulties must be questioned. Would it not be better to treat the causes of anxiety or depression through counseling or increased self-awareness rather than to depend upon pills which merely treat the symptom? Questions such as these are fundamental . . . and they are too often neglected in search of easier, but less beneficial solutions" (*Health Care Ethics,* 356).

The individual Christian should also face certain questions. While some modern drugs have brought needed relief to truly sick people, and under that aspect can be considered gifts of God, they have also attracted relatively normal people to a "drug-solution" way of life. The stress, tension, and anxiety of modern life are very real problems for many people. But is the use of drugs the best way to cope with these problems? Does not stewardship ask us to look at our life-style, our false values, our hedonistic pursuits? Does it not call us to a more simple, balanced, free way of life? The ready use of drugs can allow us to avoid very important moral questions.

Nontherapeutic drugs are those that are used for purposes of pleasure, self-transcendence, recreation and the like. People seek through drugs a feeling of relaxation, elation, happiness. Two drugs that are legally and socially acceptable are *alcohol* and *tobacco*.

The use of *alcohol* is widespread in our society. Many people have come to believe that alcohol is necessary for a good time. Alcohol is a powerful drug. Taken in sufficient quantity, it has serious effects on the body and mind. The Catholic moral teaching on alcohol has traditionally said that of and by itself the use of alcohol is neither morally right nor morally wrong. For some people, alcohol taken in moderation is relaxing and healthful. The moral problem comes from the *abuse* of alcohol, that is, drinking to excess, drinking to the point of losing control of one's physical and mental capacities. Drunkenness is morally wrong. "Let us live honorably as in daylight; not in carousing and drunkenness . . ." (Romans 13:13).

While some people knowingly and freely abuse alcohol and therefore commit sin, *the alcoholic drinks out of compulsion.* Alcoholism is a sickness which affects body, mind, and soul. The alcoholic is addicted to or dependent on the drug. Alcoholism is a widespread sickness, embracing some ten million people in the United States and affecting millions of others who are relatives, friends, or employers of the alcoholic. Space prevents a longer discussion of alcoholism here, but information and help are as close as the nearest group of Alcoholics Anonymous. AA has a proven plan for treating alcoholism. This admirable program has been instrumental in rescuing millions of people from the disease of alcoholism and returning them to a free and productive way of life.

Tobacco is a widely used drug. In recent years the evidence has been mounting that smoking, especially cigarette smoking, is dangerous to health. Good stewardship certainly demands that this danger to health and life be confronted by the Christian addicted to nicotine.

A number of nontherapeutic drugs are illegal. This includes marijuana, cocaine, heroin and the like. The greatest problem with the "hard drugs" is the danger of addiction and the whole range of behavior it brings with it. Marijuana is not considered one of the hard drugs, but the evidence seems to be growing that its deleterious effects upon the body are much greater than previously thought. Even those who favor the legalization of marijuana seem not to question the health danger. Some young people have been sold a bill of goods about the so-called "harmlessness" of marijuana. The medical evidence seems not to support such a viewpoint.

The Christian who takes seriously his or her stewardship of life and health will certainly approach all drugs with genuine prudence. If addicted, he or she will take the painful steps to freedom from the addiction.

Nuclear War and Christian Conscience

Serious consideration of the fifth commandment, "You shall not kill," moved the early Christians to ask a basic question: "In a world of violence and injustice, is there any way that a Christian can legitimately defend himself or herself when attacked by others?" In other words, is there a moral justification for self-defense?

The answer that developed may be stated in the following way: The biblical prohibition of killing refers to the *unjust* killing of an *innocent* human being. A person who unjustly attacks another in a serious way is no longer innocent. It is permitted, therefore, to defend one's own life and that of others by exerting as much force as necessary to stop the aggressor, even to the point of killing the aggressor if that is necessary for self-defense.

In light of this teaching on self-defense, a further question gradually emerged: "Does a *nation* have the right to defend itself against unjust aggression?" Considering that war involves many evils, especially the killing of other human beings, is it possible to justify war from a Christian viewpoint? The answer to this question developed into what is commonly called "the just war theory."

In the fifth century, Saint Augustine developed a very simple approach to the morality of war (though the war he was talking about was probably more like a "police action"). Saint Thomas Aquinas, in the thirteenth century, organized the thoughts of Augustine and others into a neat package. Saint Thomas said that three things were necessary for a war to be just: "First, the authority of the sovereign by whose command the war is to be waged. For it is not the business of the private individual to declare war . . . Secondly, a just cause is required, namely that those who are attacked should be attacked because they deserve it on account of some fault . . . Thirdly, it is necessary that the belligerents should have a right intention, so that they intend the advancement of the good, or the avoidance of evil . . ." It can also be drawn from the teaching of Saint Thomas that a fourth condition is necessary: namely, the right use of means or the moral conduct of the war itself.

These four conditions for a just war (lawful authority, just cause, right intention, right use of means) were developed and explained by theologians after Thomas and who lived in quite different conditions. In modern times, Pope Pius XII spoke at great length and with great regularity about these conditions in the light of modern warfare. For twenty years Pope Pius XII dedicated his Christmas message to questions of war and peace. It is safe to say, I believe, that the teachings of Pius XII were the dominant influence on the Second Vatican Council's treatment of war.

Pius XII insisted that the only "just cause" for modern war would be as a means of self-defense when all else has failed. War can be justified, therefore, only when it is absolutely necessary as a means of self-defense against a very grave injustice that touches a free community of people, and provided that this injustice cannot be halted by any other means. He insisted that "the war of aggression" was clearly immoral. "Every war of aggression is a sin, a crime, an outrage against the majesty of God, the Creator and Governor of the world."

Vatican Council II acknowledged that in the present state of affairs a legitimate war of self-defense could not be ruled out. "War has not been ruled out of human affairs. As long as the danger of war remains and there is no competent authority at the international level, governments cannot be denied the right to legitimate self-defense, once every means of peaceful settlement has been exhausted" (*Church in the Modern World*, 79).

Besides insisting that war could be considered only for "an extremely grave cause" and "in self-defense" and "as a last resort," Pius XII and Vatican Council II also insisted that the actual conduct of the war must be carried out in accord with the principles of Christian morality. It is never allowable, in war or in any other human activity, to use evil means to obtain a good end. This means that the use of all weapons must be subject to moral control. Indiscriminate destruction of whole cities or areas is morally wrong. The rights of the innocent and noncombatants must be carefully safeguarded. In the apt summary of Archbishop John Quinn (July 2, 1982), "No means of defense can be morally used which indiscriminately kills combatants and noncombatants, which devastates whole populations, or which once activated escapes human control."

The most urgent question today is: Can this updated just war theory be applied to nuclear war? It is safe to say that there is no one Catholic answer to that question, but many Catholic answers. These answers have become evident in particular reference to a pastoral letter of the American bishops on peace and war: *The Challenge of Peace: God's Promise and Our Response* (May 3, 1983).

There are many people who feel that the just war theory simply cannot be applied to nuclear war. It is simply not possible, they are saying, to use nuclear weapons in such a way as to safeguard the basic moral norms mentioned above. Is it not unrealistic to think that the awesome power of nuclear weapons can be used in a controlled and truly limited way? that the rights of noncombatants will be strictly safeguarded? that due proportion between benefit and harm done will be weighed?

A growing number of people seem to be saying that the Church must speak with a prophetic and passionate voice *against* nuclear war. Making nuanced moral judgments about nuclear war only gives it a veneer of rationality which it does not deserve. Bishop Walter Sullivan summed up the dominant feelings of these people when (in reference to the aforementioned pastoral letter) he said: "I would like to save the bishops lots of time. Their letter should simply say no to nuclear weapons, no to their use, no to their manufacture, no to their deployment and no to their existence."

There are other people who believe that the just war theory, as updated, can be applied to nuclear war. For example, a well-known philosopher writes: "Nuclear weapons are not of their very nature immoral. They can be controlled, they can be directed against military installations and personnel, and they can be used in accord with the principle of double effect, which allows direct attack against combatants but permits only incidental harm to noncombatants" (*Fagothey's Right & Reason*).

The bishops' letter on peace and war acknowledges this diversity of opinion and admits that people of good will may differ as to whether nuclear weapons may be employed under any conditions. It is clear that if nuclear weapons may be used at all, they may be used only after they have been used against our own country or our allies, and, even then, only in an extremely limited, discriminatory manner against military targets. The bishops seriously challenge the assumption that nuclear war can be limited (II, C, 3).

On the burning issue of deterrence, the bishops offer a very nuanced moral position. Deterrence, not as an end in itself but as a step on the way toward a progressive disarmament, may still be judged morally acceptable (II, C, 3).

At the same time the bishops emphasize that a *temporary* toleration of some aspects of nuclear deterrence must not be confused with approval of such deterrence. Every effort must be made to bring about the limitation and reduction of nuclear arms. While it cannot be said that the only Christian option is unilateral disarmament, it also cannot be assumed that the possession of nuclear weapons can be indefinitely justified in the name of peace.

Vatican Council II spoke strongly about the arms race. The message is more urgent now than when first given. "Undoubtedly, armaments are not amassed merely for use in wartime. Since the defensive strength of any nation is thought to depend on its capacity for immediate retaliation, the stockpiling of arms which grows from year to year serves, in a way hitherto unthought of, as a deterrent to potential attackers . . . Whatever one may think of this form of deterrent, people are convinced that the arms race, which quite a few countries have entered, is no infallible way of maintaining real peace and that the resulting so-called balance of power is no sure and genuine path to achieving it . . . Therefore, we declare once again: the arms race is one of the greatest curses on the human race and the harm it inflicts on the poor is more than can be endured" (*Church in the Modern World*, 81).

In the age of nuclear weapons, the question of *conscientious objection* arises with greater urgency. Vatican Council II endorsed those laws that "make humane provision for the case of conscientious objectors who refuse to carry arms, provided that they accept some form of community service" (*Church in the Modern World*, 79). The American bishops have challenged the laws of our country for providing "only for those whose reasons of conscience are grounded in a total rejection of the use of military force" and have asked that similar consideration be given those "whose reasons of conscience are more personal and specific" (*Human Life in Our Day)*. In a matter of such great significance, conscience must surely be respected.

Shortly after his recuperation from gunshot wounds, Pope John Paul II spoke to a group of pilgrims in these words: "Let us promise each other that we will work tirelessly for disarmament and for the abolition of all nuclear weapons." It is easy for the average person to become fatalistic about the arms race and to throw up his or her hands in a kind of despair. Yet there *are* some things that all of us can do "to wage peace."

First, we can all pray. Prayer may not seem like a very dramatic step, but it is an important one. If we believe that God is all-powerful and that he cares about his people, if we believe that God can bring sanity out of madness and good out of evil, then we must express that faith in prayer. The arms race may well be the kind of evil that can be driven out "only by prayer" (see Luke 9:29). One form of prayer that is especially appropriate for peace is the rosary. Our Lady of Fatima made that one of her specific requests.

Secondly, it is helpful to join with others who stand against nuclear proliferation and for arms limitation. It is encouraging to know that people all over the world share these values. (I personally am a member of Pax Christi, U.S.A., an organization which strives to promote peace and justice at home and abroad.)

Thirdly, it is necessary to see and crush the "seeds of war" that are planted in our own hearts. Thomas Merton wrote: "Instead of loving what you think is peace, love other men and love God above all. And instead of hating people you think are warmakers, hate the appetites and the disorder in your own soul, which are the causes of war. If you love peace, then hate injustice, hate tyranny, hate greed — but hate these things in *yourself,* not in another" (*Seeds of Contemplation).*

In short, the ringing call of the Gospel to conversion and prayer must be heard with new enthusiasm in the nuclear age.

Capital Punishment: Right or Wrong?

Several months ago I received a letter from a young woman named Debbie. She asked a very important question in these words: "Is the death penalty 'murder by society'? Our priest said in a sermon that the Old Testament taught, 'An eye for an eye,' but in the New Testament Jesus preached to 'turn the other cheek.' I'm confused. What are the views of the Catholic Church regarding capital punishment?"

I tried to respond to Debbie's letter in a brief but adequate way. Following are the basic elements of my response.

The moral debate about capital punishment has been going on for centuries. There have been, and are now, sincere people on both sides of the debate. There are certain areas of agreement and certain areas of disagreement. It is noteworthy that the American bishops have addressed this issue on a number of occasions in the past ten years. Here I will try to summarize the major points of their position.

Catholic teaching has for centuries accepted *in principle* that the state has the right to take the life of a person proven guilty of a very serious crime. Some theologians seriously question this right, but I believe it is fair to say that there is a general agreement on this basic principle.

But, *in practice,* in the concrete circumstances of modern society, is capital punishment morally justified? Should it actually be used? Here there is disagreement. Some Catholics (as well as other citizens) would say *yes.* In fact, according to opinion polls I have seen, the *majority* of Americans are in favor of capital punishment. Others, however, would say *no.* They are strongly opposed to capital punishment and believe its use should be completely abolished.

The American bishops state the question this way: "Allowing for the fact that Catholic teaching has accepted the principle that the state has the right to take the life of a person guilty of an extremely serious crime, and that the state may take appropriate measures to protect itself and its citizens from grave harm, nevertheless, the question for judgment and decision today is whether capital punishment is justifiable under present circumstances" (*Capital Punishment,* 1980).

The American bishops declare themselves *opposed* to capital punishment. I want to indicate the basic reasons why they have taken this position. It may seem that I am "stacking the deck" in favor of the bishops' position. My belief is that by reflecting on these reasons we will all be in a better position to understand what the debate is all about.

Let us start with the principle that punishment of any kind, since it involves the deliberate infliction of evil on another, needs justification. The three justifications traditionally advanced for punishment are: (1) *retribution:* that is, reestablishing the balance of justice, vindicating the rights of the offended; (2) *deterrence:* that is, forewarning others who might be tempted to commit the same kind of crime; and (3) *reform:* that is, rehabilitating the criminal and restoring him to society.

It is evident that *reform* cannot serve as a justification of capital punishment. The opportunity is taken away when the death penalty is effected.

Does *deterrence* serve as a justification for capital punishment? The bishops say: "Empirical studies in this area have not given conclusive evidence that would justify the imposition of the death penalty on a few individuals as a means of preventing others from committing crimes. There are strong reasons to doubt that many crimes of violence are undertaken in a spirit of rational calculation which would be influenced by a remote threat of death.'' In short, the bishops do not believe that capital punishment is an effective deterrent.

Does *retribution* serve as a justification of capital punishment? The bishops respond, ''We grant that the need for retribution does indeed justify punishment. But the practice of punishment both presupposes a previous transgression against the law and involves the involuntary deprivation of certain goods. But we maintain that this need does not require nor does it justify taking the life of the criminal, even in cases of murder.'' The bishops suggest that there are other ways in which the criminal justice system could bring about retribution and still protect the rights of the public.

The bishops then offer ''serious considerations which should prompt Christians and all Americans to support the *abolition* of capital punishment.'' Some of these considerations are ''*evils* present in the practice of capital punishment itself,'' while others involve ''important *values* that would be promoted by the abolition of this practice.''

First, the *evils* cited by the bishops:

1. The death penalty extinguishes any possibility of the individual's reform or rehabilitation. The person executed has no opportunity to make some creative compensation for the evil he has done.

2. The possibility of mistaken identity or the mistaken use of capital punishment is a horrifying thought. The mistake cannot be corrected.

3. Long, unavoidable delays diminish the effect of capital punishment and create long periods of anxiety in the criminal and family.

4. Executions still attract great publicity, much of it unhealthy, and stir up bitter debate in society.

5. There is evidence that the application of the death penalty is unfair and discriminatory; those condemned to die are almost always poor and are disproportionately black.

Finally, let me mention the Christian *values* that would be promoted by the abolition of the death penalty:

1. Abolition sends a message that we can break the cycle of violence, that we need not take a life for a life, that we can envisage more humane and more hopeful responses to the growth of violent crime.
2. Abolition of capital punishment is also a manifestation of our belief in the unique worth and dignity of each person from the moment of conception, a creature made in the image and likeness of God. It is particularly important that this belief be affirmed at this time in our society.
3. Abolition of the death penalty is further testimony to our conviction, a conviction we share with the Judaic and Islamic traditions, that God is indeed the Lord of life.
4. We believe that the abolition of the death penalty is most consonant with the example of Jesus, who both taught and practiced the forgiveness of injustice. . . .

Each of these points could be developed at some length, but even the simple statement of them shows the important matters at stake in capital punishment. The bishops conclude: "We recognize that many citizens may believe that capital punishment should be maintained as an integral part of our society's response to the evils of crime, nor is this position incompatible with Catholic tradition . . . We urge them to review the considerations we have offered which show both the evils associated with capital punishment and the harmony of the abolition of capital punishment with the values of the Gospel."

CHAPTER NINE
THE SIGNIFICANCE OF SEX AND CHASTITY

Sexuality: God's Gift

Life itself is the most basic gift of God to human beings, the necessary source and condition of every human activity and of all society. The human person is endowed, however, with many other gifts as well. One of the greatest is the gift of sexuality. "According to contemporary scientific research, the human person is so profoundly affected by sexuality that it must be considered as one of the factors which give to each individual's life the principal traits that distinguish it" (*Declaration on Sexual Ethics,* 1).

In reflecting on sexuality, it is helpful to keep in mind a distinction frequently made by modern theologians: the distinction between *sexuality* and *genitality*. Sexuality is the way of being and relating to the world as a male or female person. Men and women, in every aspect of living, experience themselves and others and, indeed, the entire world in a distinctly male or female way. Genitality, on the other hand, refers to the physical, organic expression of sexuality through the act of intercourse and those acts naturally related to it.

In a remarkable pastoral letter, Bishop Francis J. Mugavero underlined the deep theological meaning of sexuality when he wrote: "It is that aspect of personhood which makes us capable of entering into loving relationships with others. Theology teaches that relationship — the gift of oneself to another — is at the very heart of God. The Father and the Son give themselves totally to one another and the mutuality of their total response in love is the Holy Spirit, binding them together. We honor God and become more like him when we create in our lives the loving, other-centered relationships which at the same time give us such human satisfaction and personal fulfillment . . . Sexuality is so much more than genital activity. It is an aspect of personality which lets us enter into other persons' lives as friends and encourages them to enter our lives. The dimension of sexuality must be developed by all men and women not only because it is, as we have just seen, a gift making us more like God but is also so very necessary if we are to follow Jesus' command to become 'lovers.' It is a relational power which includes the qualities of sensitivity, understanding, warmth, openness to persons, compassion, and mutual support. Who could imagine a loving person without these qualities?'' (*Sexuality: God's Gift,* 1976).

This positive view of sexuality has not always and everywhere been emphasized in the Christian tradition. There are several dark streams which run through the bright waters of Christianity. One of the streams has shown up in the form of various *isms* (for example, Manichaeism, Jansenism). Its basic message is that there are two equal and opposing principles, one of good and one of evil. Spirit is good; matter is evil. In this view, the human body is not one of God's masterpieces, but one of his failures; the human body is evil. Sexuality is not a gift of God but an unfortunate appendage, a necessary evil. Even today many people seem to think that the only authentic Christian view is that the body is evil, sex is shameful, sin is everywhere.

This viewpoint is clearly contrary to God's gracious creative plan. ''Then God said: 'Let us make man in our image, after our likeness . . . God created man in his image; in the divine image he created him; male and female he created them . . . God looked at everything he had made, and he found it very good . . .'' (Genesis 1:26-31). What God has found very good we should not find very bad! The appropriate response to God's gift is gratitude and appreciation.

Strangely enough, however, there is another stream which flows in the opposite direction. It too has been expressed in *isms* (Hedonism, Epicureanism), but its fundamental philosophy is that the body and all its cravings are so good that nothing should ever be denied them, that bodily and genital pleasures should be sought for their own sake, and that no limitation or control should ever be placed on them. This philosophy shows up in the ''sexual revolution'' of our generation, which sponsors complete freedom for all sexual activities, no matter how dehumanizing or promiscuous they may be. It is the *Playboy* and *Playgirl* philosophy of sex.

Such a philosophy is also opposed to God's gracious plan. ''Do you not see that your bodies are members of Christ . . . you must know that your body is a temple of the Holy Spirit . . . You are not your own. You have been purchased, and at a price. So glorify God in your body'' (1 Corinthians 6:5-20). Our bodies are good, our sexual powers are good, but they are not autonomous nor are they completely independent of the moral law. Because they are gifts of God, and because they have great significance in human relationships, they come under the dominion of God. We have received them ''in trust'' from God. We are called to exercise responsible stewardship over them.

That stewardship expresses itself through the virtue of chastity. Chastity, like charity, is one of the signs by which a Christian should be known.

The Challenge of Chastity

A good case can be made that the natural virtue of chastity has been present in every known society. This does not imply that all societies have agreed on what is morally right or wrong in the sexual-genital sphere, but that some self-moderation and regulation is necessary. Sean O'Riordan, C.SS.R., has written: ''Man is by nature a sexual being, endowed with specifically sexual desires or drives. Some regulation of his sexual appetite is required by the nature of human life, both personal and social. When self-moderation and self-regulation in sexual life are apprehended and practiced by man as inherently right or good, they assume a moral character and become the natural virtue of chastity'' (*New Catholic Encyclopedia*).

It seems fairly common for people to think of chastity as merely a *negative* virtue. According to Catholic teaching, it is much more than that. ''It is aimed at attaining higher and more positive goals. It is a virtue which concerns the whole personality, as regards both interior and exterior behavior . . .'' (*Declaration on Sexual Ethics*, 11). ''Let us say clearly and without apology that chastity is a virtue which liberates the human person," writes Bishop Mugavero. "Chastity means simply that sexuality and its physical, genital expressions are seen as good in so far as we make them serve life and love." The challenge of chastity is the challenge to mature Christian love.

The New Testament issues a call to chastity. In the teaching of Jesus, chastity, like all morality, is a matter of the heart. " . . . Hear me, all of you, and try to understand. Nothing that enters a man from outside can make him impure; that which comes out of him, and only that, constitutes impurity. Let everyone heed what he hears! . . . Wicked designs come from the deep recesses of the heart: acts of fornication, theft, murder, adulterous conduct, greed, maliciousness, deceit, sensuality, envy, blasphemy, arrogance, an obtuse spirit. All these evils come from within and render a man impure" (Mark 7:14-16,21-23). Chastity is not merely an external propriety, a Victorian correctness. It touches the heart. "You have heard the commandment, 'You shall not commit adultery.' What I say to you is: anyone who looks lustfully at a woman has already committed adultery with her in his thoughts" (Matthew 5:27-28).

Chastity is a characteristic mark of the follower of Christ. "Be imitators of God as his dear children. Follow the way of love, even as Christ loved you . . . As for lewd conduct or promiscuousness or lust of any sort, let them not even be mentioned among you; your holiness forbids this. Nor should there be any obscene, silly, or suggestive talk; all that is out of place. Instead, give thanks. Make no mistake about this: no fornicator, no unclean or lustful person — in effect an idolater — has any inheritance in the kingdom of Christ and of God. Let no one deceive you with worthless arguments. These are sins that bring God's wrath down on the disobedient; therefore have nothing to do with them" (Ephesians 5:1-7). As in Paul's time, so now: We hear a lot of deceptive arguments about sexuality and the Christian moral life!

Chastity is not the greatest of the Christian virtues. Charity is. But chastity is intimately related to Christian holiness, one of the gifts of the Holy Spirit. "It is God's will that you grow in holiness: that you abstain from immorality, each of you guarding his member in sanctity and honor, not in passionate desire as do the Gentiles who know not God . . . God has not called us to immorality but to holiness; hence, whoever rejects these instructions rejects not man, but God who sends his Holy Spirit upon you" (1 Thessalonians 4:3-5,7-8).

Chastity is a demanding virtue because it is concerned with powerful, sometimes chaotic, forces in the human person. Lust is one of the capital vices, because, as Saint Thomas says, its goal is venereal (sexual-genital) pleasure and this pleasure is very desirable both because of its intensity and because of the "pull of concupiscense" deriving from original sin. Even deeply committed Christians have experienced the schizoid intensity of lust, which at times seems to have "a mind of its own." Saint Paul's vivid description of the painful conflict between the law of his mind and the law of sin which holds him captive, has application here: "I cannot even understand my own actions. I do not do what I want to do but what I hate . . . This means that even though I want to do what is right, a law that leads to wrongdoing is always ready at hand" (Romans 7:15,21).

For good people, the danger of *discouragement* may indeed be the greatest danger in pursuing the virtue of chastity. It should be emphasized that while there has often been a harsh emphasis in Catholic theology concerning sins of the flesh, this is not by any means the only legitimate emphasis. There is a great need for patience, understanding, growth in the area of sexuality. The Church, while acknowledging and insisting upon the objective order of morality in sexual matters, also acknowledges: "It is true that in sins of the sexual order, in view of their kind and their causes, it more easily happens that free consent is not fully given; this is a fact that calls for caution in all judgment as to the subject's responsibility. In this matter it is particularly opportune to recall the following words of Scripture: 'Man looks at appearances but God looks at the heart' (1 Samuel 16:7)" (*Declaration on Sexual Ethics,* 10).

Though demanding, chastity is also a liberating virtue. It sets us free from the dehumanizing lusts which we experience. It frees us from the slavery of self-centeredness. Paul recognized there was a way out of his painful inner conflict. "The law of the spirit, the spirit of life in Christ Jesus, has freed you from the law of sin and death" (Romans 8:2). Paul invites his listeners not to be discouraged by the struggle against "the wiles of the devil," but to stand firm in watchful prayer and self-denial. To be sure, the virtue of chastity does not just grow like Topsy; it needs careful cultivation. And so, "the faithful of the present time, and indeed today more than ever, must use the means which have always been recommended by the Church for living a chaste life. These means are: discipline of the senses and the mind, watchfulness and prudence in avoiding occasions of sin, the observance of modesty, moderation in recreation, wholesome pursuits, assiduous prayer and frequent reception of the sacraments of Penance and the Eucharist. Young people especially should earnestly foster devotion to the Immaculate Mother of God, and take as examples the lives of the saints and other faithful people, especially young ones, who excelled in the practice of chastity" (*Declaration on Sexual Ethics,* 12).

The virtue of chastity, far from being merely a wet-blanket kind of virtue, is one that attracts to humanity's deepest aspirations: "This virtue increases the human person's dignity and enables him or her to love truly, disinterestedly, unselfishly and with respect for others" (*Declaration on Sexual Ethics,* 12). Chastity applies to every Christian, but to each according to his or her state in life. We will now briefly review how the virtue of chastity applies to married life and single life, and respond to some common questions.

Chastity in Marriage

In chapter 7 we drew a brief "portrait of Christian marriage." We saw that marriage was described by Vatican Council II as "an intimate partnership of life and love." We recalled that Christian marriage is characterized by unity and fidelity. Above all, we emphasized that Christian marriage is a sacrament and that Jesus abides with the couple so that they will love each other with enduring fidelity.

The sixth commandment, "You shall not commit adultery," is designed to preserve mutual fidelity in marriage. Adultery is clearly a direct attack on the faithful love that is at the heart of Christian marriage. Bernard Häring, C.SS.R., thus summarizes the teaching of the Church on adultery: "The whole Judeo-Christian tradition, and especially the New Testament, condemns adultery as one of the gravest sins. If both partners in the sin are married, grave injustice is done to two marriages. It is also the sin of adultery for both partners if an unmarried person breaks into another's marriage. By adultery, the truth of the sexual act is thoroughly betrayed. It is falsity in view of the sacrament, in view of love, and in view of the meaning of sexual intercourse'' (*Free and Faithful in Christ*).

But if adultery is an attack on marriage, mutual and faithful *love* is the cement that holds marriage together and makes it constantly grow stronger. Married love has many rich dimensions. "Married love is an eminently human love because it is an affection between two persons rooted in the will and it embraces the good of the whole person; it can enrich the sentiments of the spirit and their physical expression with a unique dignity and ennoble them as the special elements and signs of the friendship proper to marriage" (*Church in the Modern World*, 49).

In a healthy marriage this love is expressed in countless ways: through a smile, a hug, an encouraging word, a helping hand. Marriage involves sexual love in the wide sense discussed above: a special kind of friendship, understanding, warmth, compassion, support. On the testimony of many couples, it is precisely this kind of healing and sustaining love that is lacking in so many marriages. Couples today, answering demands on every side, often enough sadly discover that they have failed to respond to the love needs of their spouse.

But married love is also expressed in and through the sexual-genital act of intercourse that is proper to marriage. This act is of great importance to every marriage. In Christian marriage it is indeed an outward sign of all the love the couple have for each other, all the love they possess "in Christ." The Church places great value on the sexual exchange of marriage. "Married love is uniquely expressed and perfected by the acts proper to marriage. Hence the acts in marriage by which the intimate and chaste union of the spouses takes place are noble and honorable; the truly human performance of these acts fosters the self-giving they signify and enriches the spouses in joy and gratitude" (*Church in the Modern World*, 49).

Yet sexual intercourse in marriage is not autonomous; it falls under the law of God. According to the teaching of the Church, the sexual-genital acts of marriage have an inner meaning and purpose built into their very nature by the Creator God. In the words of Pope Paul VI, the individual couple is not "free to proceed completely at will, as if they could determine in a wholly autonomous way the honest path to follow; but they must conform their activity to the creative intention of God, expressed in the very nature of marriage and its acts, and manifested by the constant teaching of the Church" (*Humanae Vitae*, 10).

This teaching, the pope explained, "is founded on the inseparable connection, willed by God and unable to be broken by man on his own initiative, between the two meanings of the conjugal act: the unitive meaning and the procreative meaning . . . By safeguarding both these essential aspects, the unitive and the procreative, the conjugal act preserves in its fullness the sense of true mutual love and its ordination toward man's most high calling to parenthood" (*Humanae Vitae*, 12).

This statement embraces a very basic moral principle about marital intercourse: the inseparable connection between the unitive (love-giving) and procreative (life-giving) meanings of the act. Two fundamental conclusions flow from this principle. Both are stated in *Humanae Vitae:*

First, "a conjugal act imposed upon one's partner without regard for his or her condition and lawful desires is not a true act of love, and therefore denies a demand of right moral order in the relationships between husband and wife." While there are multiple levels of motivation in the sexual exchange of marriage, the spouses must make every effort to eliminate selfishness and hostility from their relationship. Pope John Paul II in one of his weekly talks on sexuality in 1980, startled the world by saying that a husband can be guilty of lust with his wife "if he treats his wife only as an object to satisfy his own instinctive needs." A loveless sexual act is sinful.

Secondly, according to Pope Paul VI, "each and every marriage act must remain open to new life." As a consequence of this principle, "every action which, either in anticipation of the conjugal act, or in its accomplishment, or in the development of its natural consequences, proposes, whether as an end or a means, to render procreation impossible" must be excluded as a licit means of regulating births (14).

This teaching on contraception has been a matter of public debate and personal anguish in the Church for some fifteen years. It is not possible here to review the debate, but it is necessary to place this teaching in its proper context. The proper context includes three other moral principles taught by the Church: (1)

responsible parenthood; (2) natural family planning; (3) persevering effort. A few words about each of these points:

Responsible parenthood involves a prayerful discernment of many factors in the life of an individual couple. Vatican Council II expresses it this way: "Married couples should regard it as their proper mission to transmit human life and to educate their children; they should realize that they are thereby cooperating with the love of God the Creator and are, in a certain sense, its interpreters. This involves the fulfillment of their role with a sense of human and Christian responsibility and the formation of correct judgments through docile respect for God and common reflection and effort; it also involves a consideration of their own good and the good of their children already born or yet to come, an ability to read the signs of the times and of their own situation on the material and spiritual level, and, finally, an estimation of the good of the family, of society and of the Church. It is the married couples themselves who must in the last analysis arrive at these judgments before God. Married people should realize that in their behavior they may not simply follow their own fancy but must be ruled by conscience — and conscience ought to be conformed to the law of God in the light of the teaching authority of the Church, which is the authentic interpreter of the divine law" (*Church in the Modern World*, 50).

Such a responsible discernment may uncover serious reasons why a couple should space out the births of their children. The Church does not oppose such a responsible conclusion. In fact, Pope Paul VI points out that "the Church teaches then that it is licit to take into account the natural rhythms immanent in the generative functions, for the use of marriage in the infertile periods only, and in this way to regulate birth without offending the moral principles which have been recalled earlier" (*Humanae Vitae*, 16).

Natural family planning deserves the serious attention of every couple. There are a number of misunderstandings about it. On the theoretical level, some people say it is "just another method of contraception and not unlike some of the others." On the practical level, a number of couples seem to think that it is far too complicated for the average couple to use, and not very effective.

In regard to the first objection, Pope John Paul II, as indeed popes and theologians before him, is at pains to show the *difference* between contraception and natural family planning. The basic difference is that natural family planning respects the inseparable connection between the unitive and procreative meanings of human sexuality, and contraception does not respect it. Pope John Paul II comments: "It is a difference which is much wider and deeper than is usually thought, one which in the final analysis involves two irreconcilable concepts of the human person and of human sexuality. The choice of the natural rhythms involves accepting the cycle of the person, that is, the woman, and thereby accepting dialogue, reciprocal respect, shared responsibility and self-control. To accept the cycle and to enter into dialogue means to recognize both the spiritual and corporal character of conjugal communion and to live personal love with its requirement of fidelity . . . In this way sexuality is respected and promoted in its truly and fully human dimension and is never 'used' as an 'object' that, by breaking the personal unity of body and soul, strikes at God's creation itself at the deepest level of the deepest interaction of nature and person" (*Family*, 32).

In regard to the second objection, it is not possible to discuss here all the practical aspects of natural family planning. Some people seem not to realize that the new techniques of natural family planning are far superior to the "calendar rhythm" of twenty years ago. Almost every diocese is able to provide couples with up-to-date information. There is ample evidence that any average couple, with goodwill and basic instruction, can make natural planning work. And there are many good reasons for a couple to adopt this approach to responsible parenthood. Some of these reasons are succinctly described by Benedict M. Ashley, O.P., and Kevin D. O'Rourke, O.P.: "(1) When properly practiced, it can be as effective as any method except sterilization and it does not have the obvious disadvantages of a sterilizing operation. (2) Unlike other comparably effective methods, that is, progesterones and intrauterine devices, it has no medical risks. (3) It is never abortifacient as progesterones and intrauterine devices almost always are. (4) It is inexpensive and does not require regular medical checkups in order to avoid side effects, but can be effectively taught by simple instruction" (*Health Care Ethics*, 279).

Finally, it seems important, even at this date, to emphasize the gentle compassion and loving encouragement of Pope Paul VI toward struggling couples. "We do not at all intend to hide the sometimes serious difficulties inherent in the life of Christian married persons; for them, as for everyone else, 'the gate is narrow and the way is hard, that leads to life' . . . Let married couples, then, face up to the efforts needed, supported by the faith and hope which 'do not disappoint . . . because God's love has been poured into our hearts through the Holy Spirit, who has been given to us'; let them implore divine assistance by persevering prayer; above all, let them draw from the source of grace and charity in the Eucharist. And if sin should still keep its hold over them, let them not be discouraged, but rather have recourse with humble perseverance to the mercy of God, which is poured forth in the sacrament of penance. In this way they will be able to achieve the fullness of conjugal life . . ." (*Humanae Vitae*, 25).

The call to holiness which married couples have received is at times a demanding call. "It will be easier for married couples to make progress if, with respect for the Church's teaching and with trust in the grace of God, and with the help and support of the pastors of souls and the whole ecclesial community, they are able to discover and experience the liberating and inspiring value of the authentic love that is offered by the Gospel and set before us by the Lord's commandment" (*Family*, 34).

Chastity in Single Life

Sexual-genital relations find their proper and beautiful place in marriage. And, according to the Christian tradition, still upheld by almost all of the Christian churches, these relations find their proper place *only* in marriage. The American bishops summarize this tradition well: "Our Christian tradition holds the sexual union between husband and wife in high honor, regarding it as a special expression of their covenanted love which mirrors God's love for his people and Christ's love for his Church. But like many things human, sex is ambivalent. It can be either creative or destructive. Sexual intercourse is a moral and human good only within marriage; outside marriage it is wrong" (*To Live in Christ Jesus*, 19).

This teaching was recently emphasized by the Vatican's *Declaration on Sexual Ethics* which said in part: "Today there are many who vindicate the right to sexual union before marriage, at least in those cases where a firm intention to marry and an affection which is already in some way conjugal in the psychology of the subjects require this completion, which they judge to be connatural . . . This opinion is contrary to Christian doctrine, which states that every genital act must be within the framework of marriage . . . This is what the Church has always understood and taught and she finds a profound agreement with her doctrine in men's reflection and in the lessons of history" (7).

While there are still many young people who are firmly resolved to abstain from sexual relations before the full celebration of their marriage, there are others who justify "living together" or "having sex" as long as "nobody gets hurt." But the "getting hurt" is the problem. Often enough the hurt shows up only in the course of time. Sexuality is a fundamental dimension of the human *person,* not merely of the human body. Persons can be hurt in many ways. The expression of sexuality in genital relations is far from being a mere biological act surrounded by pleasant sensation. It involves the innermost personality.

In his insightful personalistic way, Pope John Paul II emphasizes this point: Sexuality "is realized in a truly human way only if it is an integral part of the love by which a man and a woman commit themselves totally to one another until death. The total physical self-giving would be a lie if it were not the sign and fruit of a total personal self-giving, in which the whole person, including the temporal dimension, is present: If the person were to withhold something or reserve the possibility of deciding otherwise in the future, by this very fact he or she would not be giving totally" (*Family*, 11).

The pope's emphasis on "the total self-giving would be a *lie* if . . ." throws the spotlight on the deepest meaning of sexual-genital relations. Sexuality is a kind of language, a way of communicating truth. It is a special kind of language because by its very nature it is meant to express something special to another person. Bishop Mugavero explains it this way: "In truthful human communication we must accept the meaning which is present in certain actions. A warm smile and a tender embrace are universal signs of friendship; to communicate in a human way is to be true to the meaning of a sign when I use it in my life. As much as they might like to do so, no couple can rewrite the meaning of sexual intercourse. It is tied to committed love; it is tied to life-giving. When a person engages in sexual intercourse it is a sign of giving one's very self, whether one intends to or not. To let my actions be a sign of self-gift if my heart knows the truth to be different is to lie" (*Sexuality: God's Gift*).

Richard McCormick, S.J., also speaks directly to this question: "The question that must be put to our generation is this: In what circumstances should the sexual experience of intimacy occur if sexual language is to retain its viability as truly human language? . . . The answer given by Christians to the question . . . is simply this: sexual expression is the language of relationship. It gets its full human meaning from the relationship it expresses and fosters. And the relationship which provides us with our best opportunity to integrate and humanize our sexuality is the covenant relationship of marriage; for it is friendship that generates constancy, loyalty, fidelity. And these are the qualities that allow sex to speak a truly human language" (*Notes on Moral Theology 1965-1980*).

The whole truth of sexuality is made possible only in marriage. It is a mistake for people to think of marriage as only a fancy ceremony or a "piece of paper." "The institution of marriage is not an undue interference by society or authority, nor the extrinsic imposition of a form. Rather, it is an interior requirement of the covenant of conjugal love which is publicly affirmed as unique and exclusive in order to live in complete fidelity to the plan of God, the creator. A person's freedom, far from being restricted by this fidelity, is secured against every form of subjectivism or relativism and is made a sharer in creative wisdom" (*Family*, 11).

There is no doubt that our society gives encouragement to casual and even exploitative sexual relations. But casual sex by definition means being indifferent to the personal needs and feelings of another as well as becoming callous toward one's own feelings. There are many ambiguities connected with the language of sex. It *can* be a way of expressing anger, frustration, selfishness, even hatred and raw domination of another. A person who has given himself or herself to another with the understanding that there was love and commitment can be deeply hurt, and hurt for life, if he or she discovers that the other was in effect playing around. This type of deceptive sex goes on constantly and many people are hurt by it.

Our culture places heavy pressure on unmarried people. They can be made to feel that there is something wrong with them if they avoid genital sex before marriage. Yet the virtue of chastity is proposed to us by a Church, a community, which has been a faithful guide to men and women for nearly two thousand years.

That Church, reflecting the spirit of Christ, tells us that chastity *is* possible and in the long run the best teacher of the complex language of sexuality and love. It reminds us, moreover, that chastity is a gift of the Holy Spirit who stands ready to give that gift to all who truly desire it.

Chastity: Common Questions

In this chapter we have reviewed some of the basic teachings of the Church on sexuality and chastity. There are, of course, many other urgent questions in this important area of human life. Here we want to take a brief look at four common questions. Because of space limitations, it is not possible to afford these questions the thorough treatment they deserve, but at least we can indicate the moral teaching of the Church as it applies to each.

Q. *What is the Church's teaching on masturbation?*

This teaching was explained at some length in the Vatican's *Declaration on Sexual Ethics,* 8. There are two basic aspects to the teaching: the *objective* morality of the act and the *subjective* moral responsibility. On the first point the Declaration says: "Both the Magisterium of the Church — in the course of a constant tradition — and the moral sense of the faithful have declared without hesitation that masturbation is an intrinsically and seriously disordered act. The main reason is that, whatever the motive for acting in this way, the deliberate use of the sexual faculty outside normal conjugal relations essentially contradicts the finality of the faculty. For it lacks the sexual relationship called for by the moral order, namely the relationship 'which realizes the full sense of mutual self-giving and human procreation in the context of true love.' All deliberate exercise of sexuality must be reserved to this mutual relationship."

Having established this moral principle, the Declaration then addresses some of the subjective aspects of responsibility: "On the subject of masturbation modern psychology provides much valid and useful information for formulating a more equitable judgment on moral responsibility and for orienting pastoral action. Psychology helps one to see how the immaturity of adolescence (which can sometimes persist after that age), psychological imbalance or habit can influence behavior, diminishing the deliberate character of the act and bringing about a situation whereby subjectively there may not always be serious fault. But in general, the absense of serious responsibility must not be presumed; this would be to misunderstand people's moral capacity.''

Q. *What is the Church's teaching on homosexuality?*

The Church's teaching is explained in a number of documents. A key distinction seems to be made between homosexual orientation and homosexual activity. There is also an emphasis on the civil and ecclesial rights of the homosexual person. The American bishops explain the Church's teaching in this way: ''Some persons find themselves through no fault of their own to have a homosexual orientation. Homosexuals, like everyone else, should not suffer from prejudice against their basic human rights. They have a right to respect, friendship and justice. They should have an active role in the Church community. Homosexual activity, however, as distinguished from homosexual orientation, is morally wrong. Like heterosexual persons, homosexuals are called to give witness to chastity, avoiding, with God's grace, behavior which is wrong for them, just as nonmarital sexual relationships are wrong for heterosexuals. Nevertheless, because heterosexuals can usually look forward to marriage, and homosexuals, while their orientation continues, might not, the Christian community should provide them with a special degree of pastoral understanding and care'' (*To Live in Christ Jesus*, 19).

Q. *What is the Church's teaching on artificial insemination by donor?*

In 1949 Pope Pius XII expressed the Church's teaching in this way: ''Artificial insemination in marriage, but produced by the active element of a third party, is immoral and as such to be condemned outright. Only marriage partners have mutual rights over their bodies for the procreation of new life, and those rights are exclusive, nontransferable, inalienable.'' In 1951 the same pope explained at greater length: ''To reduce cohabitation and the conjugal act to a simple organic function for the transmission of seed would be converting the home, the sanctuary of the family, into a mere biological laboratory . . . The conjugal act is a personal act, a simultaneous and immediate cooperation on the part of the husband and wife. It is, by the very nature of the persons involved and the propriety of the act itself, an expression of the mutual gift which according to the Holy Scripture brings about union in one flesh only. This is much more than the union of seeds brought about artificially, without the natural action of husband and wife. The marital act, in its natural setting, is a *personal* act of cooperation, the right to which husband and wife give each other when they marry.''

Another aspect of "donor insemination" concerns *the child* who is conceived in this way. Pope Pius XII observed: "Nature imposes on those who give life to a small child the task of its preservation and education. But between marriage partners and a child that is the fruit of the active element of a third person — even if the husband consents — there is *no bond of origin, no moral or juridical bond of conjugal procreation.*''

Q. *What is the Church's teaching on celibacy?*

Celibacy "for the sake of the kingdom of God" holds an honored place in the teaching of the Church, as it did in the teaching of Christ (see Matthew 19:12). Vatican Council II refers to it as "an exceptional gift of grace," "a special symbol of heavenly benefits," and "a most effective means of dedicating oneself to the divine service and the works of the apostolate" (*Religious Life*, 12). Those who are called to the state of celibacy should respond generously and faithfully.

The Church is also concerned that celibacy not be viewed as a rejection or contradiction of Christian marriage and its values. Pope John Paul II expresses in a beautiful way the relationship between marriage and celibacy: "Virginity or celibacy for the sake of the kingdom of God not only does not contradict the dignity of marriage but presupposes it and confirms it. Marriage and virginity or celibacy are two ways of expressing and living the one mystery of the covenant of God with his people. When marriage is not esteemed, neither can consecrated virginity or celibacy exist; when human sexuality is not regarded as a great value given by the creator, the renunciation of it for the sake of the kingdom of heaven loses its meaning . . . In virginity or celibacy, the human being is awaiting, also in a bodily way, the eschatological marriage of Christ with his Church, giving himself or herself completely to the Church in the full truth of eternal life. The celibate person thus anticipates in his or her flesh the new world of the future resurrection. By virtue of this witness, virginity or celibacy keeps alive in the Church a consciousness of the mystery of marriage and defends it from any reduction or impoverishment" (*Family*, 16).

CHAPTER TEN
JUSTICE FOR ALL

Material Possessions: The Teaching of Jesus

Money plays an important part in everybody's life. There is no escape from the need for some material possessions in human life. And even beyond the necessities of food and shelter and clothing, there seems to be an urge in human nature toward the acquisition of material things.

Knowing human nature as he did, Jesus often addressed himself to the basic questions of material goods and our attitudes toward them. The Gospel offers many striking examples of the teaching of Jesus. His words invite us to think deeply about money, material possessions — and especially about our personal attitudes toward them.

To be sure, it is difficult to formulate a balanced view of the teaching of Jesus on material goods. We always run the risk of watering down some of his very hard sayings. On the other hand, we also run the risk of reading our own pet ideas into the Scriptures. So it is helpful if we can stand back, as it were, and take an honest look at what the Scriptures say to us about these matters.

In the first place, Jesus did not condemn out of hand the possession and use of material goods. In the famous passage about the birds of the air and the lilies of the field, Jesus quite directly acknowledges our need for food and clothing. ''. . . Your heavenly Father knows all that you need'' (Matthew 6:32). The urgent concern of Jesus seems to be with the *attitude* of his listeners toward these things. He challenged those who were so worried about their material needs. "Stop worrying, then, over questions like, 'What are we to eat, or what are we to drink, or what are we to wear?' The unbelievers are always running after these things. Your heavenly Father knows all that you need. Seek first his kingship over you, his way of holiness, and all these things will be given you besides" (Matthew 6:31-34).

Jesus points out the great pitfall of letting material goods become the be-all and end-all of our lives. "Remember, where your treasure is, there your heart is also" (Matthew 6:21). We can easily become slaves to money and all that money can buy. "No man can serve two masters . . . You cannot give yourself to God and money" (Matthew 6:24). As he usually does when speaking of morality, Jesus emphasizes first the inner attitude, the heart. It is the heart that matters!

In popular Jewish belief at the time of Jesus wealth was often considered *a sign of God's favor.* If you were good and righteous, God would reward you by conferring wealth on you! Wealth was a visible sign of your acceptance by God. Jesus exploded this myth. ". . . only with difficulty will a rich man enter into the kingdom of God . . . it is easier for a camel to pass through a needle's eye than for a rich man to enter the kingdom of God" (Matthew 20:23-24).

Jesus here challenges the illusion, still widespread, that somehow money makes a person morally good. What easily happens is that wealth makes a person feel *independent* of God and of others. "Avoid greed in all its forms. A man may be wealthy, but his possessions do not guarantee him life." The rich farmer who was so smug about his wealth and so self-centered would hear God say: "You fool! This very night your life shall be required of you. To whom will all this piled-up wealth of yours go?" On this Jesus comments: "That is the way it works with the man who grows rich for himself instead of growing rich in the sight of God" (Luke 12:15,20,21).

Jesus said it was *hard* for the rich to enter the kingdom of God, but not impossible. The disciples (as is clear from the story of the rich young man) were aware that many of their contemporaries did consider wealth a sign of God's favor. When Jesus denied this, they concluded that practically no one could be saved. Jesus replied that with God's help it was possible for the rich to be saved if they, like the poor, recognized their dependence on God for their salvation.

The more one reflects on the teaching of Jesus about money, the more does one see how his commandment of love comes into play. Jesus' "new commandment" was certainly not meant to be vague and other-worldly. Jesus himself spoke in dramatic terms about sharing the ordinary things of life (food, water, clothing, companionship) with those in need. In his description of the Last Judgment, he *identifies* himself with those in need: ". . . I assure you, as often as you did it for one of my least brothers, you did it for me" (Matthew 25:40).

Certainly the early Christian community understood the teaching of Jesus in this very practical way. They took responsibility for one another. "They would sell their property and goods, dividing everything on the basis of each one's need" (Acts 2:45). The law of love extended to the nitty-gritty needs of daily life. They looked on their wealth not as something to be hoarded, not as something to be defended at all costs, but as something to be shared with others. The problem is not so much the possession of wealth as the right *use* of it.

It would seem, then, that Jesus calls his followers to a change of heart, a new attitude about the place of material possessions in their lives. Wealth is to be used for the needs of oneself, one's family, others in need. Money is in service to justice and charity. And you can't take it with you!

Theft and Fraud: Faces and Masks

The seventh commandment, "You shall not steal," brings us face-to-face with a very important Christian virtue: the virtue of justice. Not only is justice important, it is also very extensive. It touches our lives at many points and in many ways. Over the centuries Christian scholars have put labels on various kinds of justice and the demands they make on us.

One of the most basic forms of justice is called *commutative* justice: that is, the virtue by which one person renders to another that which is his or her due or the virtue which urges us to give to others what is theirs by right.

Catholic moral teaching on commutative justice starts with a general orientation. It can be stated this way: All the things of the earth belong to God who created them. God has ultimate dominion over all created things. According to his plan, created goods are for the use of all people. So that the goods of this earth may truly serve their purpose, God has endowed human beings with certain basic rights.

One of these rights is the right to own private property. "Private ownership," according to Vatican Council II, "or some other kind of dominion over material goods provides everyone with a wholly necessary area of independence, and should be regarded as an extension of human freedom" (*Church in the Modern World*, 71). In almost the same breath, however, the Council adds that private property is not an absolute right. "By its very nature, private property has a social quality deriving from the communal purpose of earthly goods. If this social quality is overlooked, property often becomes an occasion of greed and disturbances" (71). (We shall return to this aspect when treating of social justice.)

Understood in this way, private ownership is the foundation of commutative justice. We naturally expect others to respect what rightfully belongs to us, and we in turn must respect what is theirs. This is where the seventh commandment, "You shall not steal," clearly applies.

Theft (or stealing) may be defined as the secret taking of another's goods against his or her reasonable wishes. It is "secret" because if a person gives permission we aren't talking about theft. It is "against his or her reasonable wishes" because there can be occasions when the extreme need of one person renders the protection of superfluous goods by another unreasonable. (See *Church in the Modern World*, 69.)

Most Christians have grown up with the idea that out-and-out theft is immoral. But stealing, especially in modern societies, wears many masks. For all practical purposes, the following fall under the definition of theft: borrowing an article without the owner's consent, taking goods as a loan but refusing or neglecting to return them, running up a charge account when one has no reasonable expectation of being able to pay, living extravagantly while burdened with debts and the like.

In addition, the person who keeps what he or she finds without trying to discover the owner is little better than a thief. The person who accepts as a gift what he or she knows to be stolen property, or sells it, is as morally wrong as the original thief. To deceive another in matters of property (for example, by lying or giving short weight in selling), to do sloppy work when one is paid for a standard job, to use faulty material when one is paid for good material, to claim more wages than one has actually worked for, to hold back wages for work completed — all of these are really forms of stealing and fall under the Lord's commandment.

Unjust damage to the property of others is also contrary to the seventh commandment. This includes damage done to the property of other individuals, obviously, but also damage done to public property — for example, defacing or mutilating books or art objects of a public library. Taking "souvenirs" from restaurants and motels, and other such practices, are often politely defended. But no matter how we mask such practices, stealing is their real name.

The seventh commandment also prohibits *fraud*. Or, to put it positively, this commandment directs us to be honest in the fulfilling of all *contracts*. A contract is a mutual agreement entered into by two or more persons to do or not to do certain things. A number of basic conditions are necessary for a valid contract.

These conditions may be briefly described as follows: (1) The agreement must be *externally* manifested in some way. (2) All parties must give *free* consent. (3) A serious *mistake* or substantial *error* on the side of any party renders the contract null and void. (4) The object of a valid contract *cannot be* something morally wrong. In addition to these basic conditions, there are often other particular conditions placed on contracts by civil or ecclesiastical law. A person entering a contract would naturally try to discover all of the conditions that are binding.

According to Catholic moral teaching, contracts bind our consciences under the virtue of commutative justice. In demanding that we respect the rights of others, justice clearly demands that we fulfill all valid contracts. Fraud is the great enemy here. Fraud may be defined as deception or trickery by which the contractual rights of another are harmed. There are, unfortunately, numerous examples of fraud in modern society.

For example, fraud often shows up in the contracts of *buying and selling*. Fraud is present when the truth is suppressed or a lie is told. In selling things, one has the moral right to a just price only; that is, the price that corresponds to the *value* of the commodity being sold. While it is assuredly difficult in all circumstances to pinpoint a just price, it is not difficult to spot price-gouging or the taking advantage of the young or ignorant or poor to demand an exaggerated price. (This is the kind of sin that cries to heaven for vengeance!)

The seller is obliged to reveal all substantial defects in the thing sold. Thus, to sell a home knowing that the foundation is seriously defective, but refusing to disclose this fact, is a clear act of injustice. It stands to reason, of course, that if a buyer has been informed of a defect and wishes to buy anyway, the seller is not guilty of injustice. What we are saying here is that the popular expression "let the buyer beware" *(caveat emptor)* is *not* a good moral principle.

Advertising is another area where fraud is all too common. Advertising is a necessary and legitimate enterprise in modern societies. Some ads are truthful, tasteful, informative, and even funny. But some are not. Ads which contain falsehoods and ads that deliberately communicate a false impression are against justice.

Another place where fraud is all too common is in *insurance contracts*. An insurance contract is one whereby, in return for a fixed payment, the insurer guarantees the insured that a certain sum will be paid for a specified loss. The insurance policy sets down the exact conditions of the contract. The insurer is morally obliged to cover the insured when the conditions of the contract are fulfilled. The insured person is morally obliged to submit truthful information (for example, age, health condition) and to make only truthful claims against the insurer.

The examples of theft and fraud given in this section could easily be multiplied. Even people who consider themselves committed Christians can begin to take these violations of the seventh commandment for granted. This commandment is worthy of our deepest reflection, for its violation dehumanizes all of us and makes our society more and more subject to the power of evil. What Saint Paul said to the Ephesians applies to all of us: "The man who has been stealing must steal no longer . . ." (Ephesians 4:28).

Obligation to Restore

Not only should the person who has been stealing "steal no longer," but he or she should also be ready to make *restitution*. Restitution means giving back to the rightful owner what does not belong to us; it means restoring stolen goods or their equivalent.

Restitution obliges whenever commutative justice has been violated.

The Scriptures speak clearly of the obligation to restitution. In the Book of Ezekiel we read the word of the Lord: "And though I say to the wicked man that he shall surely die, if he turns away from his sin and does what is right and just, giving back pledges, restoring stolen goods, living by the statutes that bring life, and doing no wrong, he shall surely live, he shall not die" (Ezekiel 33:14-16).

The New Testament highlights the story of Zacchaeus. When the word got around that Jesus was going to stay at Zacchaeus' house, people began to say, "He has gone to a sinner's house as a guest." But Zacchaeus defended himself in these words: ". . . I give half my belongings, Lord, to the poor. If I have defrauded anyone in the least, I pay him back fourfold" (Luke 19:8).

Saint Augustine, with his great gift for summarizing basic truths, wrote: "Restitution is necessary for the forgiveness of sins against justice. If the sinner does not restore something that he can restore, he does not have repentance but only a facsimile."

Most Catholics are aware of the fact that sins against justice can be absolved in the sacrament of Penance only on the condition that the penitent promises to make necessary retribution. Since some cases of justice can be very complex, it is suggested that individual questions be brought to one's confessor. In general, however, we can point out that restitution obliges us: (1) when we have unjust *possession* of another's property; and (2) when we have caused unjust *damage* to another's property.

Concerning unjust possession of another's property, let us note the following examples:

- If I *knowingly* have in my possession another's property, I must restore it at once to its proper owner.
- If I have used it or given it away, I must restore the *equivalent* to the proper owner.

Concerning unjust damage to another's property, I am bound to make restitution or reparation when the following three conditions are present:

- My act was strictly unjust.
- My action was the real and effective cause of the damage.

- My action was deliberately unjust (not simply an unavoidable accident).

Finally, the following conditions also apply in making restitution:

- I should try to make restitution to the person whose right was violated. If that is not possible, I should make it to his or her family. If I do not know the identity of the person, I should make it to the poor.
- It is permissible to make restitution anonymously; I need not endanger my good name by public acknowledgment of my injustice.
- I should make restitution as soon as possible.

Moral Responsibilities of Employees

Some time ago I received an interesting letter from a young man. Part of the letter read as follows: "A few evenings ago, I was involved in a long and interesting debate about many areas of right and wrong. The discussion finally settled on what I would call the duties of employees toward employers. I've been wondering if there is a handy moral code somewhere about these matters."

Since his question was a good one and since his moral concerns touch many of our lives, I responded to him through the *Dear Padre* Sunday Bulletin, published by Liguori Publications. It might be helpful to other readers if I include my basic response to the young man here.

I am not sure if there is "a handy moral code" about the duties of employees, but perhaps I can help by stating three basic principles of justice that apply to employees and some examples which may make these principles more practical.

The first principle is this: *Employees are bound in conscience to work conscientiously and fairly in return for their wages.* Here are some examples of how this principle is violated:

— by those who loaf away hour after hour in idle conversation with fellow workers or on the telephone with friends;
— by those who use much of their on-the-job time in taking care of personal or family business;
— by those who extend the lunch period or coffee break to unreasonable limits.

The second principle is: *Employees are bound in justice to respect the property rights of their employers*. Think of the many ways in which this principle may be transgressed:

— by those who take for their own use and benefit goods and materials that rightfully belong to their employers (though this is sometimes referred to as one of America's favorite indoor sports, it is still stealing; the practice of taking things may range from office supplies, such as pencils or paper clips, to expensive materials, such as steel, lumber, electrical equipment and the like);

— by those who neglect to take reasonable care of the equipment and material they make use of in the performance of their jobs;

— by those who pad their expense account, demanding recompense for expenses not actually incurred.

The third principle is this: *Employees are bound in justice to respect the good name and reputation of their employers*. More often than people think, this obligation is set aside:

— by those who have gained knowledge of their employers' past life or secret sins and spread this knowledge far and wide for no good reason;

— by those who tell lies about their employers in order to justify themselves, or who exaggerate small faults into monstrous crimes.

It may seem at first glance that these principles are too basic. It is true, of course, that many tricky situations arise in the workaday world, but I believe that these basic principles of justice do provide a "handy moral code" for most employees, especially if an employee is willing to examine his conscience in an honest and critical way.

One of the great moral problems that all of us face is the "moral environment" in which we live and work. If our fellow employees tend to downgrade moral principles and to take advantage of the company or the boss whenever they can, that will usually have a negative effect on our behavior. We have to struggle to offset that negative influence and be faithful to our Christian principles at work as well as at home.

I once received a small plaque from a friend of mine who shared my admiration for one of our great popes, Pope Leo XIII. Almost a hundred years ago, Pope Leo spoke of the moral responsibilities of employees. The plaque reminded the employee:

> To perform entirely and conscientiously
> Whatever work has been freely and equitably agreed upon;
> Not in any way to injure the property
> Or harm the person of my employer.

That in itself may be about as good a "handy moral code" as we are likely to find anywhere.

Moral Responsibilities of Employers

After the above letter and my response appeared in the *Dear Padre* Bulletin, I received another letter. This is what it said: "I was angered when I read, 'Is there a handy moral code for employees?' What about the other side of the coin? You laid it on the line for employees, so now lay it on the line for employers. They aren't angels, you know."

I responded to this letter in the following way.

It is certainly true that employers have moral obligations toward their employees. This fact arises from the very nature of the contractual relationship between the employer and employee. The employee has certain basic rights which must be respected by the employer. Though this matter is complicated, I will try to highlight several basic principles of social justice that clearly apply to employers. (For a full treatment, see Pope John Paul II's extensive encyclical letter *On Human Work*, 1981.)

The first principle is this: *The employer is morally bound to respect the human dignity of his or her employees*. This principle may seem so basic that there is no need to mention it. Yet Pope John Paul II insists that this principle — "the primacy of persons over things" — is the most important principle of all.

Some concrete requirements flow from this principle: such as the obligation of employers to provide a work environment that is not harmful to the employees' physical health or moral integrity, and the obligation not to impose more work than human strength can endure, nor the kind of work that is unsuited to a worker's age or sex.

The second principle is this: *The employer is bound in justice to pay the employee a just wage*. Pope John Paul II reaffirms the traditional teaching of the Church on this matter: "The key problem of social ethics in this case is that of remuneration for work done. In the context of the present there is no more important way of securing a just relationship between the worker and the employer than that constituted by remuneration for work" (*On Human Work*, 19).

Many complex questions arise about this moral obligation. We cannot attempt to treat all of them here. There are, however, certain general guidelines that flow from the moral teaching of the Church:

- The minimum just wage should be determined by the very reason why a person works — namely, to earn a livelihood.
- The just wage must take into consideration the requirements of the *family*. In the words of Pope John Paul II: "Just remuneration for the work of an adult who is responsible for a family means remuneration which will suffice for establishing and properly maintaining a family and providing security for its future" (*On Human Work*, 19).
- Women employees have a right to receive equal wages for equal work.

The third principle is: *The employer has a moral obligation to provide basic social benefits intended to ensure the life and health of employees and their families.* Pope John Paul II emphasizes three basic benefits: "The expenses involved in health care, especially in the case of accidents at work, demand that medical assistance should be easily available for workers and that as far as possible it should be inexpensive or even free of charge. Another area regarding benefits is the area associated with the right to rest. In the first place this involves a regular weekly rest comprising at least Sunday, and also a longer period of rest, namely, the holiday or vacation . . . A third area concerns the right to a pension and to insurance for old age and in the case of accidents at work" (*On Human Work*, 19).

By and large, our society accepts these moral principles and to a great extent insists on them by law or government regulation. We know from the sad pages of history that the relationship between employer and employee has not always been a smooth and cooperative one. Christian employers and employees are called to witness to Gospel values in the marketplace. In the words of Vatican Council II: "Human activity proceeds from man: it is also ordered to him. He learns, he develops his faculties, and he emerges from and transcends himself. Rightly understood, this kind of growth is more precious than any kind of wealth that can be amassed. It is what a man is, rather than what he has, that counts'' (*Church in the Modern World*, 35).

The Call to Social Justice

The virtue of justice is like a rainbow that contains the colors of the spectrum, which at times seem to merge one into the other. While it is fairly easy to define commutative justice, it is harder to define *social* justice. It has been described and defined in many ways. For our purposes here, we can say that social justice is that virtue which urges the individual member of a social group to seek the common good of the whole group rather than just his or her own individual good.

For a hundred years, beginning with the pontificate of Pope Leo XIII (1878) the modern popes have tried to awaken in Catholics a "social conscience." In the words of Pope Pius XII, a social conscience "calls individuals to their social duties, urges them to take into account in all their activities their membership in a community, to be preoccupied with the welfare of their neighbors and with the common good of society."

This social or community sense is at the heart of social justice. It is a constant reminder to us that we are *social* beings, that we *need* society, that social living is essential for our full humanity.

A social conscience expresses itself through the virtue of social justice. Social justice is concerned with the *organization* of society so that all the members of the society can share in the common good. It urges each member of the society to act in an organized way to cure the ills of society. The individual person, however, often feels helpless in the face of serious social problems, such as those concerned with economic, industrial, racial, and political relations.

Because no one listens to the isolated voice, as Pope John XXIII expressed it, the modern popes have strongly encouraged professional groups, labor unions, farmers' associations, and the like. People need to have a sense of solidarity with others, a feeling of mutual support and guidance, the strength that comes from shared effort. Social justice calls us to our responsibility to contribute to the common good and to oppose unjust violations of the common good. It tells us that we must seek fairness in social relationships and oppose what is unfair. But it also implies that we can do this best by uniting with others in a *common* effort. In a word, social justice encourages us to organize with others to bring about a better society.

But social justice, according to the modern popes, must go further. It is not enough to organize for a better society. There is need to make our *social institutions* reflect the basic values of justice and charity. Our life in society is made up of institutions designed to bring about harmony and order in our relationships with one another. Thus, the school is an educational institution, the labor union is an economic institution, the government is a political institution. Social institutions touch our lives constantly — when we choose a school, look for a job, build a home, vote in an election. Even if we wanted to, we could not avoid social institutions in our lives.

These institutions affect our moral life, exert pressure on us, urge us to think this way or that, choose this or that. Social justice prompts us to measure these institutions: Are they just? Are they fair to all? Do they enhance the dignity of the human person? Do they foster the values of the Judaeo-Christian morality on which this nation was built?

The American bishops touch on a very important point when they say: "In a pluralistic society, religiously neutral public institutions and structures cannot be expected to embody the beliefs of any one religious group, nor indeed should they reflect an anti-religious view of life. They can and should help create the conditions in which values flourish in human lives and persons committed to Christian goals can pursue them without hindrance, without squandering their rights, and with full opportunity to transmit their principles to future generations" (*To Live in Christ Jesus*, 37).

As Christians, it is our responsibility to work for the reform of institutions which no longer reflect authentic moral values. It is our responsibility to do what we can to breathe into these social institutions the spirit of justice, truth, and charity.

False attitudes such as "I can't be bothered . . ." "That's their problem, not mine . . ." "Don't ask me to get involved . . ." are clearly opposed to the virtue of social justice. The rugged individualism of the storied West is hardly a badge of the follower of

Christ today. In the words of Vatican Council II, "There is a kind of person who boasts of grand and noble sentiments but lives in practice as if he could not care less about the needs of society." But the Christian today is called to overcome this "merely individualistic morality. For," the Council continues, "the best way to fulfill one's obligations of justice and love is to contribute to the common good according to one's means and the needs of others, even to the point of fostering and helping public and private organizations devoted to bettering the conditions of life" (*The Church in the Modern World*, 30).

The late Bishop James Rausch once said that, in the light of Vatican Council II's document *The Church in the Modern World* and in light of the Synod of Bishops' document *Justice in the World* (1971), "it is no less important for the Church to be doing the work of social justice every day than it is for us to provide the celebration of the Eucharist or to preach the Gospel." Though startling at first sight, that statement is true. For, as the Synod itself taught, "Christian love of neighbor and justice cannot be separated. For love demands an absolute commitment to justice, namely, a recognition of the dignity and rights of one's neighbor" (*Justice in the World*, 34).

The Cry of the Poor

One of the burning issues of social justice is the gap that exists between the rich and poor. Pope Paul VI, surely one of our greatest popes, frequently asked wealthy and middle-class people to listen to the "cry of the poor." He said: "You hear rising up, more pressing than ever, from their personal distress and their collective misery, the cry of the poor."

In every society, and ours is certainly no exception, the cry of the poor can be heard: children crying because they do not have enough to eat, the sick crying because they cannot afford adequate health care, the elderly crying because their income cannot be stretched any further, parents crying because they cannot provide for their children.

Pope Paul VI raised the question that must be faced by every Christian: "How will the cry of the poor find an echo in your lives?" He says pointedly, "in *your* lives," because each one of us who professes to be a follower of Christ has a responsibility to listen to the cry of the poor and to respond to it.

But what can we do? Pope Paul outlined a three-point program in answer to that question. Briefly, let us reflect on these three points.

1. The cry of the poor will lead us to make *social justice* real in our lives. Or, to put it negatively, it will stop us from being involved in any form of social injustice. As we saw in our previous section, we are called to "awaken our consciences" to the demands of social justice. Lip service is not enough; we must *live* by the principles of social justice. We must stand *for* human dignity and the fundamental rights of the human person. We must stand *against* unjust institutions and structures wherever we find them.

2. The cry of the poor will not allow us to be carried away by an uncurbed seeking of material possessions. In a world saturated by material goods, from expensive luxuries to throw-away gadgets, we must examine our life-style. In a society where some people are smothered by more material possessions than they can ever use, while others lack the basic necessities of life, we must decide what our moral principles really are. Are we, too, not called to Gospel simplicity?

3. The cry of the poor will urge us to share our goods and possessions with others. Here, above all, as the bumper sticker says, if we are not part of the solution, we are part of the problem! The teaching of Christ and the Church in this regard is a "hard saying," one from which many people turn away. Pope Paul VI took pains to explain it clearly: "To quote Saint Ambrose, 'You are not making a gift of your possessions to the poor person. You are handing over to him what is his. For what has been given in common for the use of all, you have arrogated to yourself. The world is given to all, and not only to the rich.' That is, private property does not constitute for anyone an absolute unconditional right. No one is justified in keeping for his exclusive use what he does not need, when others lack necessities" (*Progress of Peoples*, 23).

There are, of course, many ways in which we can share with the poor. Some people prefer to share one-on-one, which can be a very personal way of doing it. Others prefer to share through an established community or Church organization. Cooperation among different religious groups in matters of practical justice and charity is a marvelous way of practicing ecumenism.

But share we must! We cannot refuse to answer the cry of the poor and still call ourselves Christian. The Christ whom we love and serve was born poor, lived a poor life, and died poor. ". . . for your sake he made himself poor though he was rich, so that you might become rich by his poverty" (2 Corinthians 8:9). He himself describes the purpose of his mission in these words: ". . . to bring glad tidings to the poor" (Luke 4:18).

Above all, however, as we saw in our examination of the teaching of Jesus on material goods, Jesus identified himself with the hungry, the alien, the sick, the imprisoned. One of the most moving passages of the New Testament is the Last Judgment scene of Matthew's Gospel. Jesus surprises his listeners when he says, for example, "I was hungry and you gave me no food . . . ." Immediately they want to know when they saw *him* hungry and did not feed him. His response: "I assure you, as often as you neglected to do it to one of these least ones, you neglected to do it to me" (Matthew 25:42,45).

Vatican Council II's document *The Church in the Modern World* eloquently concludes with this thought: "Christians can yearn for nothing more ardently than to serve the men of this age with an ever growing generosity and success. Holding loyally to the Gospel, enriched by its resources, and joining forces with all who love and practice justice, they have shouldered a weighty task here on earth and they must render an account of it to him who will judge all on the last day" (93).

Racial and Ethnic Justice

In the rainbow of justice there are some "hidden colors": namely, racial and ethnic injustices. Many Christians even today question that racial and ethnic relations fall under the virtue of justice. Perhaps that is why the American bishops have returned to these moral questions on a number of occasions.

"The members of every racial and ethnic group are beings of incomparable worth; yet racial antagonism and discrimination are among the most persistent and destructive evils in our nation. Those victims of discrimination of whom we are most conscious are Hispanic Americans, Black Americans, and American Indians" (*To Live in Christ Jesus,* 25).

In examining the matter of racial and ethnic justice, it is helpful to distinguish several terms. One is the term *prejudice*. This word is derived from two Latin words meaning "pre-judgment," that is, a judgment passed before the evidence is considered. Although the term is used in a variety of ways, we are here concerned with it primarily as manifesting an attitude of mind based not on objective reasons but upon emotional states, such as fear, anger, frustration, or jealousy.

Most of the time prejudices are not deliberately formed. Very often they are learned in childhood and are derived from the attitudes and statements of parents, relatives, teachers, companions. In relatively few cases, they result from personal experiences.

Once formed, prejudices are extremely difficult to change. The reason is that very often a person does not even realize that he or she is prejudiced. He or she accepts particular prejudices without question as the truth. When prejudices are deeply rooted, it does little good to present evidence to the contrary in the form of rational arguments, statistics, or personal experience.

A second important term in this discussion is *discrimination*. By this we mean the unjust and unequal treatment of equal human beings. Racial discrimination may be defined as the unjust and unequal treatment of individual human persons, not because of their faults or failings or their lack of ability or merit, but simply because they are members of a certain race. Discrimination, therefore, usually results from prejudice. Nevertheless, a person may have deep feelings of prejudice, which he cannot easily overcome, and *yet never indulge in conscious discrimination of any kind*. The real moral problem, then, is in racial discrimination or racism.

Vatican Council II underlined the basic moral teaching of the Church when it said: "All men are endowed with a rational soul and are created in God's image; they have the same nature and origin and, being redeemed by Christ, they enjoy the same divine calling and destiny; there is here a basic equality between all men and it must be given greater recognition . . . Undoubtedly not all men are alike as regards physical capacity and intellectual and moral powers. But forms of social or cultural discrimination in basic personal rights on the grounds of sex, race, color, social conditions, language or religion, must be curbed and eradicated as incompatible with God's design" (*The Church in the Modern World*, 29).

The American Catholic bishops, in their pastoral letter on racism (1979), speak even more directly: "Racism is a sin: a sin that divides the human family, blots out the image of God among specific members of that family, and violates the fundamental human dignity of those called to be children of the same Father. Racism is the sin that says some human beings are inherently superior and others essentially inferior because of race. It is the sin that makes racial characteristics the determining factor for the exercise of human rights."

The bishops point out that through good laws, strictly enforced, our society has made some progress in racial justice. While it is true that laws may not be able to change attitudes, they can at least deter those who might otherwise seek to violate the rights of others. However, we are far from final success. "For example, the principles of . . . proportionality and restraint have sometimes been violated in law enforcement within our nation. Racial justice in such areas as housing, education, health care, employment, and the administration of justice must be given high priority. The Church, too, must continue efforts to make its institutional structures models of racial justice while striving to eliminate racism from the hearts of believers . . ." (*To Live in Christ Jesus*, 27).

The quest for racial justice is part of the larger search for social justice. As we mentioned earlier, every Christian has a stake in that struggle. It is true that not every individual Christian can be accused of racial discrimination, but that does not absolve the individual from all responsibility. "We must seek to resist and undo injustices we have not caused, lest we become bystanders who tacitly endorse evil and so share in guilt for it" (25).

Each Christian is called to personal conversion and renewal in love and justice. Each Christian is called to join hands with others in promoting programs that have been successful in rooting out racial discrimination in our society. "There must be no turning back along the road of justice, no sighing for bygone times of privilege, no nostalgia for simple solutions from another age. For we are children of the age to come, when the first shall be last and the last first, when blessed are they who serve Christ the Lord in all his brothers and sisters, especially those who are poor and suffer injustice" (*Pastoral on Racism*, 1979).

CHAPTER ELEVEN
THE VALUES OF TRUTH AND HONESTY

The Truth Will Set You Free

Emphasizing as we often do the tender kindness and compassion of Jesus, we run the risk of forgetting his sterner side. We know how strongly he condemned the false religious views of the Pharisees. He had even stronger words of condemnation for those who deliberately twisted his words. In a powerful passage Jesus says: "Why do you not understand what I say? It is because you cannot bear to hear my word. The father you spring from is the devil, and willingly you carry out his wishes. He brought death to man from the beginning, and has never based himself on truth; the truth is not in him. Lying speech is his native tongue; he is a liar and the father of lies" (John 8:43-44).

Because the devil is the father of lies, because lying speech is his native tongue, it would follow that the disciple of Christ would have nothing to do with lying. Saint Paul expresses well this demand of discipleship: "Stop lying to one another. What you have done is put aside your old self with its past deeds and put on a new man, one who grows in knowledge as he is formed anew in the image of his Creator" (Colossians 3:9-10).

Not surprisingly, therefore, a distinct part of the moral tradition of the Church is concerned with preserving the value of truth and pointing out the evil of lying. Deliberate lying is an offense against the God of truth and therefore unworthy of a Christian. In the fifth century Saint Augustine put it this way: "Words exist, not that men may mutually deceive themselves with them, but that through them one may express his thought to another. Therefore, to use words in order to deceive and not for the purpose for which they were intended is sinful."

Without engaging in a long discussion about the exact definition of lying, we can say that there are at least two dimensions to the notion of a lie. One is that we express to another something contrary to what we believe to be true. It is "speaking against our interior convictions." The second is that we intend to deceive another person.

A number of modern theologians make a sharp distinction concerning this intention to deceive. Their view is that one may say something false to someone who has *no right to know the truth*. Bernard Häring, C.SS.R., explains: "In recent times, a number of reputable Catholic theologians have distinguished a morally justifiable false utterance from lying. Almost all hold as chief reason and as clear condition that the other party has no right to receive the accurate information and there is no other way to conceal truth although concealment is dutiful" (*Free and Faithful in Christ*). If, for example, the secret police ask me where my mother, who has done no wrong, is hiding, I can tell them straight out that I don't know. Since their intentions are evil, they have no right to know the truth. When I speak falsely to them, I am not really lying.

To get back to the morality of lying, we can see that it is morally wrong for two reasons. First of all, it is an abuse of the faculty of speech. The purpose of this faculty is to communicate our thoughts and ideas to others. By lying we pervert this faculty. Secondly, and more significantly, lying tends to erode the trust and confidence that people have in one another. The fabric of society is fragile. It is held together by delicate threads of mutual trust and confidence. The less people can trust one another, the less harmony and peace exist in society.

Certain kinds of lies — for example, *perjury* (false swearing) and *calumny* (injuring the good name of another by lies) — obviously cause great harm to the common good and to the rights of others. Clearly, there are cases when lying constitutes a grave matter against the law of God. The *pathological* liar also causes great harm in the community of which he or she is a part, though usually not with full deliberation.

Saint Paul frequently reminds us that we are all members of the Body of which Christ is the Head. He encourages us to grow to full maturity. ". . . Let us profess the truth in love and grow to the full maturity of Christ the head. Through him the whole body grows, and with the proper functioning of the members joined firmly together by each supporting ligament, builds itself up in love" (Ephesians 4:15-16). Paul sees lying (as well as other sins like anger and stealing) as breaking down the Body of Christ. "See to it, then, that you put an end to lying; let everyone speak the truth to his neighbor, for we are members of one another" (Ephesians 4:25).

As Christians, then, our ideal should be to seek the truth, to walk in the truth, to share the truth. Truth builds up the Body of Christ. Lying tears it down. Truth can set us free. Lying leads us into tangled webs. Truth deepens the image of God in us. Lying defaces it. "Then you will know the truth, and the truth will set you free" (John 8:32).

Taming the Tongue

Saint James, whose epistle is found toward the end of the New Testament, was a straight-talking moralist. Some of his most pungent observations are directed at the way people abuse the gift of speech. The gift of speech is a great and noble gift. But it is also a gift which can be easily and frequently defiled. In characteristic fashion, James lays it on the line: "If a man who does not control his tongue imagines that he is devout, he is self-deceived; his worship is pointless" (James 1:26).

James becomes almost poetic in describing how important control of the tongue is in living a Christian moral life. "When we put bits into the mouths of horses to make them obey us, we guide the rest of their bodies. It is the same with ships: however large they are, and despite the fact that they are driven by fierce winds, they are directed by very small rudders on whatever course the steersman's impulse may select. The tongue is something like that. It is a small member, yet it makes great pretensions . . ." (3:3-5).

With great insight James describes how difficult control of the tongue really is. ". . . See how tiny the spark is that sets a huge forest ablaze! The tongue is such a flame. It exists among our

151

members as a whole universe of malice. The tongue defiles the entire body . . . Every form of life, four-footed or winged, crawling or swimming, can be tamed, and has been tamed by mankind; the tongue no man can tame. It is a restless evil, full of deadly poison'' (3:5-8). It is not surprising, then, when James makes this striking statement: ''If a person is without fault in speech he is a man in the fullest sense, because he can control his entire body'' (3:2).

Abuse of the gift of speech can be aimed in many directions. It can be directed toward God: blasphemy, cursing, perjury. It can be aimed at the common good: lying, divulging secrets. It can be leveled at the welfare of our neighbor and in many different ways. To describe all of these ways would take a small encyclopedia. For our purposes, however, we want to dwell on one of these ways: namely, the destruction of the good name or reputation of others by abuses of the tongue.

''A good name is more desirable than great riches, and high esteem, than gold and silver'' (Proverbs 22:1). Few would deny this saying of Proverbs, for we are social beings. To live in society we need a good name, a reputation that is worthy of respect. It is true, of course, that some people destroy their own reputations. But it is also true that reputations are ruined by others.

Catholic moral theology has made labels for the ways in which one person can ruin the reputation of another. One way is called detraction; another way is called calumny. Both of these are violations of the eighth commandment: ''You shall not bear false witness against your neighbor.''

Detraction means making known, without a sufficiently serious reason, the hidden sins or failings of another. In detraction, what is said is *true*, but it is also secret or private. We retain our right to our good name until we forfeit it by some *publicly* known misdeed or crime. Until such time, we have the right to our reputation. Anyone who unjustly takes that right away from us commits a real injustice.

Calumny (also called slander) means the ruining of another's reputation by lies. It goes beyond detraction and is morally more offensive, since it violates justice and is contrary to the truth as well.

There is no doubt that detraction and calumny can be serious sins. The seriousness depends in part on the amount of harm done to another's reputation. But serious or light, detraction and calumny have no rightful place in the Christian's life.

The person who has unjustly taken away the good name of another is bound to make restitution for the loss of reputation and other losses which are foreseen as likely to emerge from the detraction or calumny. It is true that the damage done by detraction or calumny can frequently *not* be repaired, but a sincere conversion requires an effort to do what one can to repair the consequences of one's irresponsible behavior.

It is worth emphasizing that, just as it takes two to tango, it also takes two to have a slanderous conversation. By lending a willing ear to detraction and calumny we share in their sinfulness. While it is true that we may sometimes "get caught" in such conversations, it is also true that we ordinarily do not have to listen and are free either to change the subject or walk away.

In our more honest moments many of us would probably agree that our tongue is a "restless evil" and that most of our sins are sins of the tongue. Experience teaches, however, that we will not be able to gain control over our tongue unless we first gain control over our heart, for external actions proceed from deep within us. It is only by watching over our heart that we will ever be able to control our tongue!

In a more positive way, we should use our gift of speech to build up rather than tear down, to compliment rather than criticize, to highlight good qualities rather than focus on bad qualities. Or, as James would put it, we should use our tongue "to fulfill the law of the kingdom . . . 'You shall love your neighbor as yourself' " (James 2:8).

The Subject of Secrets

The subject of secrets has been of grave concern to moral theologians for centuries. They have recognized a moral obligation for all of us to respect the right of others to their secrets. Without a healthy respect for secrecy, they knew, there is almost always a severe loss of trust and goodwill among individuals and groups in society. Peaceful social living becomes difficult indeed when a person's secrets easily become public knowledge.

The keeping of secrets is an important moral duty of the follower of Christ. A person has as much right to his or her secrets as he or she has to personal property and reputation. The Gospel that speaks to us of justice and charity in all of our relationships surely challenges us to examine our attitude toward the secrets of others.

A secret may be defined as something known only to a certain person or persons and purposely kept from the knowledge of others. A secret is something that for one reason or another should not be made known to other people. The possessor of a secret has a moral responsibility to conceal his or her knowledge of the secret.

We can distinguish various kinds of secrets. First, there is the *natural* secret: that is, a matter which by its very nature calls for secrecy on the part of all who have knowledge of it. Certain matters which belong to one's private life or family life cannot be aired publicly without causing injury and harm to that person. For example, Jack observes over a period of many months that his neighbor Joe, a pillar of the community, gets seriously drunk every weekend. Jill, a secretary, knows from flurries of phone calls that her boss has serious personal financial problems.

Secondly, there is a *promised* secret: that is, a matter which one has promised to keep secret *after* one has become aware of it. Though the matter may not of its very nature require secrecy, one gives his or her word that the matter will be kept secret.

Thirdly, there is the *entrusted* secret: that is, a secret which one receives because of an agreement, either explicitly stated or implicitly understood, that one will keep the secret. The agreement is given *before* the secret is revealed. "I will tell you a secret provided that you will not tell anybody else." "Yes, I agree to this condition."

A very important example of the entrusted secret is a *professional* secret: that is, a secret which comes to a professional person (for example, a doctor or a lawyer) in the discharge of his or her official functions. There is, in effect, an implicit agreement between the professional and the client that what is entrusted to the professional as such is covered by secrecy.

Finally, a unique kind of secret is what Catholics commonly refer to as the *seal of confession:* that is, the secrecy demanded of the confessor in the sacrament of Penance.

The moral obligation to keep a natural secret frequently falls under the virtue of justice; its violation is usually a direct infringement of another's *rights*. It ordinarily causes harm or damage to the person concerned. It is surprising how many people who would not think of violating the property rights of their neighbors casually violate their right to secrecy.

The promised secret obliges one because one has given his or her word. The breaking of one's word, given in a promise, is a lie of the most vicious kind. Turmoil and distrust arise in a community when there is doubt if others will keep their word.

The entrusted secret is a matter of justice arising out of a professional relationship; its violation most hurts the common good. The violation of an entrusted secret erodes the confidence people have in those to whom they must confide their secrets.

Though the obligation to keep secrets is an important one, it is not absolute. At times one may, at times one must, reveal secrets. In general, the obligation to keep any type of secret ends if the matter becomes public knowledge. Moreover, if the person concerned gives permission to reveal the secret, one is no longer obliged to secrecy. This permission may be presumed when the revelation of a secret would be clearly beneficial to the one whose secret it is or when continued secrecy would prove harmful to him or her.

In addition, a secret may be revealed: (1) to avert serious harm from the one who holds the secret; (2) to protect an innocent third party; (3) to safeguard the community from danger. The common good of the many must come before the individual's right to secrecy. Thus, if I know that one person in an office, factory, or school is corrupting many individuals, I must reveal this matter to those in a position to do something about it.

In regard to the secret of confession, no reason whatever justifies the breaking of it. The confessor must be willing to die rather than reveal the confessional secret. Canon law reserves grave penalties for any confessor who would dare to do so.

The Book of Proverbs gives good advice: "Discuss your case with your neighbor, but another man's secret do not disclose; Lest hearing it, he reproach you, and your ill repute cease not. Like golden apples in silver settings are words spoken at the proper time" (Proverbs 25:9-11).

CONCLUSION

We began this book by saying that our God is The God Who Calls. In Baptism he called us to live a life of love in fidelity to Christ, to be followers of Christ.

Under the light of the moral teaching of the New Testament and of the Church, we have in these pages searched out some of what following Christ means for us today.

To follow Christ faithfully demands unselfish love and genuine service of others. It requires the carrying of the cross and authentic self-discipline. It entails a daily conversion from evil and sin and a tireless search for reconciliation. Obviously, it cannot be done without the strengthening and healing and renewing grace of God, given to us in Christ Jesus.

This way of life, this following of Christ, is a challenging adventure for the years allotted to us here on earth. It is also the beginning of the life to come, the life God has prepared for those who love him. For, in the words of Vatican Council II, ''When we have spread on earth the fruits of our nature and our enterprise — human dignity, brotherly communion, and freedom — according to the command of the Lord and in his Spirit, we will find them once again, cleansed this time from the stain of sin, illuminated and transfigured, when Christ presents to his Father an eternal and universal kingdom 'of truth and life, a kingdom of holiness and grace, a kingdom of justice, love and peace.' Here on earth the kingdom is mysteriously present; when the Lord comes it will enter into its perfection'' (*The Church in the Modern World*, 39).

In a word, the faithful follower of Christ lives a life of love now, and looks forward to a fuller and richer one forever!

INDEX

OTHER HELPFUL PUBLICATIONS
FROM LIGUORI

You and the Ten Commandments
by Russell M. Abata, C.SS.R., S.T.D.
A series of 9 booklets explaining and discussing the Ten Commandments and the place they have in modern living. $7.95.

Sexual Morality
by Russell M. Abata, C.SS.R., S.T.D.
A straightforward discussion of sex, covering such subjects as the relationship between sex and love and the need for moral guidelines. The last chapter is a beautiful essay on sex and God. $1.50.

Jesus' Pattern for a Happy Life:
The Beatitudes
by Marilyn Norquist
A beautiful, joy-filled book which invites you to consider the Beatitudes as a pattern for peace — a plan that CAN be followed in today's world. In the Sermon on the Mount, Jesus gave us a pattern for daily life in his Kingdom, a way to face troubles and problems and still find peace, hope, and joy. $2.95.

Sorting It Out with God
by Jim Auer
This book presents an understanding look at the very real problems of youth and suggests Christian approaches to these problems and ways to make Christian decisions about life-situations. $1.95.